reading and teaching

IVOR GOODSON

Studies in the
Postmodern Theory of Education

Shirley R. Steinberg
General Editor

Vol. 441

The Counterpoints series is part of the Peter Lang Education list.
Every volume is peer reviewed and meets
the highest quality standards for content and production.

PETER LANG
New York • Washington, D.C./Baltimore • Bern
Frankfurt • Berlin • Brussels • Vienna • Oxford

YVONNE DOWNS

reading and teaching
IVOR GOODSON

PETER LANG
New York • Washington, D.C./Baltimore • Bern
Frankfurt • Berlin • Brussels • Vienna • Oxford

Library of Congress Cataloging-in-Publication Data

Downs, Yvonne.
Reading and teaching Ivor Goodson / Yvonne Downs.
pages cm. — (Counterpoints: studies in
the postmodern theory of education; vol. 441)
Includes bibliographical references and index.
1. Goodson, Ivor. 2. Education—Philosophy. I. Title.
LB880.G662D69   370.1—dc23   2013013161
ISBN 978-1-4331-2017-6 (hardcover)
ISBN 978-1-4331-2016-9 (paperback)
ISBN 978-1-4539-1142-6 (e-book)
ISSN 1058-1634

Bibliographic information published by **Die Deutsche Nationalbibliothek**.
Die Deutsche Nationalbibliothek lists this publication in the "Deutsche
Nationalbibliografie"; detailed bibliographic data is available
on the Internet at http://dnb.d-nb.de/.

Cover images courtesy of Andrew Goodson at Oil Internet Limited

The paper in this book meets the guidelines for permanence and durability
of the Committee on Production Guidelines for Book Longevity
of the Council of Library Resources.

© 2013 Peter Lang Publishing, Inc., New York
29 Broadway, 18th floor, New York, NY 10006
www.peterlang.com

Printed in the United States of America

For Petar Novakovic and Hermine Novakovic (nee Giwisser), my much
loved, much missed dad and mam.

Contents

Acknowledgments

It has been a challenge and a privilege to have spent so much time with Ivor in the course of researching for and writing this book. He has been wise and generous in his reading of my reading of his life/work. To encounter him, in his writings and through other media, or face to face, is to be infected with optimism. Liz Briggs has been a star. Always cheerful, always just at the end of an email, she saved me countless hours by providing ready access to Ivor's work. I owe Pat Sikes, teacher, mentor, most loved friend, more than words can say. I am better for knowing her. James Downs has generously read innumerable drafts and when I was lost he had the knack of asking just the right question. My sons Wilf and Jonah Skinner light up my life and keep me grounded. Paul Downs was there when I needed a shoulder to cry on. He has made it a joy to be a step-mum. I value beyond measure the friendship of the girls I met at school, Belinda, Bev, Carol, Claire, Krystyna, Sue and the truly wonderful Juan. When the going got tough I focused on our next night out. Juan, who in the midst of her own sorrow thought of me, teaches me every day how to be a good person. I could never leave out my sisters and brothers, Monika, Kurt, Dušanka Elizabeth, Mark and Kristina. I am secure in their presence, even in their absence. Pamela Anderson had to share an office with me throughout the writing of this book and had the grace never to complain, though heaven knows I gave her cause. Shirley Steinberg's tacit support throughout has been invaluable as has the support of all at Peter Lang. My heartfelt thanks to you all and especially Jackie Pavlovic.

Jess Moriarty kindly gave permission to quote from her unpublished work: Autobiographical and researched experiences with academic writing: An analytical ethnodrama. University of Brighton 2012. Copyright Jess Moriarty. All rights reserved.

Liz Briggs also gave kind permission to quote from one of our personal email exchanges.

I acknowledge here also the lives of Gillian Galloway and Mark Novakovic who left us too soon.

Introduction

I want to go on living my own intellectual project.

(Goodson, 2011, p. 8)

Ivor Goodson is one of the most important thinkers and researchers on education and schooling of our times. His paper "Life Histories and the Study of Schooling" (1980–1981) rehabilitated life history methodology, establishing it as a critical approach to educational research. His book on the social construction and social histories of the curriculum, *School Subjects and Curriculum Change,* first published in 1983, secured his immediate elevation to the rank of professor, the ink on his PhD being barely dry. Since then Ivor has worked continuously and with unwavering commitment as, to use his own terms, a public intellectual. His output is prodigious. His reach, both geographically and intellectually, is awe-inspiring. He has broken fresh ground theoretically, particularly but by no means exclusively in the areas of curriculum and narrative and in conceptualizing change. Methodologically he has revitalized research agendas, insisting, for example, that including teachers and other public service professionals, their lives, dreams, and politics, is crucial to formulating, implementing, and analyzing public, particularly educational, policy. Bringing his historian's orientation to empirical research and his historian's concern for context and supporting documentation to sociological perspectives, he argues that the success, but more often the failure, of educational reform is traceable in no small way to the people who are responsible for its implementation on a daily basis. Their mediating influence is what counts in evaluations of efficacy, rather than inherent weaknesses in the constitution of the reform itself, however real these may also be. He has collaborated with many other significant contributors to the study of education and its role in fostering just societies, and many important educationists have offered commentaries on Ivor's work. He has also, in the prefaces and introductions to his works and in conversations with others, offered his own readings of his output. For all those reasons, providing (in the words of the general editors to this series) a "deeper, yet accessible conceptual framework in which to negotiate and expand" his work initially presented itself as frighteningly daunting. What could possibly be added to the enormous body of interpretation and commentary that already exists? My fears were dispelled during a meeting with Ivor to discuss the possibility that (a) this was something that could be done, (b) I might be willing to take it on, and (c) Ivor would be happy for me to do so.

Although the first point is arguably the most important, I will deal with these issues in reverse order, because Ivor's being happy for me to take it on turned out to be the easiest one to resolve, and yet it is also central to understanding and addressing the other two. Ivor did not hesitate in expressing his confidence that I would do a sterling job, grounded in the fact that we had met briefly at a conference some months before and had immediately hit it off; the "chemistry" between us was good, and there was a bond. Now, it may seem foolhardy to assign the (re)interpretation of one's life/work to date on the basis of such unscientific reasoning. But this just highlights the limitations of such reasoning. For one thing, "shrewd" is a much more accurate description of Ivor's judgment. When Jess Moriarty (2012) interviewed him, he points out the obvious fact that he would not be where he is today if he had not been "canny." More importantly, he knew I was "getting" what he was about, despite considerable differences in our biographies and histories. That we are both from what is commonly understood as a working-class background provides a strong bond of mutual comprehensibility between us. Saying we are *working class* is risky here because the term encompasses a multiplicity of lived realities. There is a danger that it glosses over rather than facilities understandings of what that means. But as Mahoney and Zmorczek (1997) claim:

> (W)hat it means to have a working class background *is* different in each case. But not so different that we do not recognise each other and not so different that our connectedness (at least on this issue) disappears. (p. 5, original emphasis)

There are powerful and enduring influences from our backgrounds that are embedded deep in our bones and within our psyches—and our hearts. One of the ways in which this manifests itself is in our resilience, something that often presents itself as a combative approach. Metaphors of war, of battle, and of fighting are embedded in Ivor's writing. If either of us had ever tried to hide our backgrounds, this kind of fighting talk would be a dead giveaway. This is not to say that Ivor is in any way aggressive. In fact he is a great romantic, although he apologizes for it when he catches himself being that way. This is not so much because he wants to fit in and romanticism in scholarly circles is not the done thing. It is because he is in constant communication with imagined dialogic others of his original community, and here romanticism can easily slip into pretension. This would invite some not inconsiderable teasing from those to whom he still owes allegiance. Where we come from, if you act in ways that might be construed as pretentious, then you are inviting others to poke fun at you. In extremis this can be a mechanism of control, but it can also take the form of good-natured teasing, and that is something Ivor obviously does enjoy.

We also knew on an intuitive level and in a visceral way that neither of us had sold out. To translate, we knew without much in the way of discussion that our loyalties were with the communities into which we were born (Ivor calls this loyalty to his "tribe"), that our life project was to address the injustices with which these communities deal on a daily basis and that even though this project takes the form of an intellectual engagement, an exercise of the mind, it is driven by the heart. The fact that I have not been as impervious to the external forces that reposition and distort the expression of those loyalties in their realization in scholarship and elsewhere, nor as steadfast in my resistance to the temptation to wander off track, only makes me appreciate all the more the achievement of someone who has remained resolutely and unwaveringly on message throughout. Establishing cause and effect is often a doomed project but I would venture to say here that Ivor's fortitude is explained by his designation of his project as a mission.

Again, even writing the word *mission* inspires uncomfortable feelings of embarrassment and self-consciousness in me. I also know that Ivor has an abhorrence of sounding "holier than thou," of pretension and pomposity, for reasons already mentioned. And yet, it is striking that when he speaks from the heart, when he sets out the fundamentals of what has motivated his life's work, he uses elevated terms and language that rarely has currency in the academy. Consider the following example taken from a conversation Ivor had with Ragna Adlandsvik, which is set out in *Life Politics: Conversations About Education and Culture* (Goodson, 2011):

> Bring back the poetic, the joy, which should be crucially part of education above all. It should be audacious, exciting, lively, vivid, vital, and all those things will make it emancipating. (p. 9)

This hardly echoes the measured language and subdued tones usually associated with academic writing and shortly after this utterance Ivor states, "I can be pompous, but I try not to be, and that is important" (p. 12). To reiterate, this abhorrence of pomposity must be read here not as an individualized predilection. Beverley Skeggs's (1997) study of working-class girls on "caring" courses in a college of further education revealed how this aversion to pretension is ingrained in working-class psyches. So the work Ivor is doing is imbued with a missionary purpose and therefore requires committed, engaged, and passionate language, but at the same time he is at pains to clarify that this does not signify his wholesale embrace of a world in which this is the lingua franca, a world that would be rejected by his tribe for its ostentation and affectedness.

Turning now to my willingness to take it on, I was torn. On the one hand I could hardly believe my luck. I had taken a special interest in Ivor's work since my first attempt at writing a life history of my own educational experiences and trajectories. I was only weeks into an MA in educational research at the University of Sheffield and had the huge good fortune to be taught by Pat Sikes, who had coauthored with Ivor a book on doing life history in educational settings (Goodson & Sikes, 2001). Pat marked my assignment, noting that "this is a good example of a life history according to the sort of model that Ivor Goodson advocates." I had not intentionally followed his lead. My approach had been more informed by Charles Wright Mills's (1959) *The Sociological Imagination* and the linking of personal biography to history because at the time I could not afford to buy the Goodson and Sikes text and the library copy was already out on loan. But I needed no persuasion that we are "in history."

My parents told me that if it had not been for "the war" (World War II) I would not be here. After the war, they had both come to work in the woolen textile mills of Huddersfield, in what was then the West Riding of Yorkshire, my Serbian dad as a displaced person and later a "naturalized" British citizen and my Austrian mum as an economic migrant. Their arguments were also explicitly framed by my dad as reenactments of Serbian struggles to throw off the yoke of Hapsburg imperialist oppression. History is air to me and so Ivor's insistence on folding history into otherwise ahistorical sociological accounts did more than strike a chord. I felt fortunate that I had a space in which to engage with his work more deeply and then, importantly, to share fresh and new understandings with others.

On the other hand, I had reservations because I was not sure there was anything fresh or new left to say to those already familiar with his work and I was concerned that this volume would have appeal only to those coming new to it, as vital as these readers are. To my mind Ivor has been absolutely consistent from the start of his intellectual involvement in the field of education, has been totally on message, in words I used earlier. In his own words, those of the quotation that opens this chapter, he has lived his intellectual project. His role as a public intellectual is profoundly informed by the person he is, which in turn reflects his continued commitment to his tribe. He alludes to loyalty to his tribe in some way in almost everything he writes. For me a striking example is when he tells Ragna Adlandsvik (Goodson, 2011) about meeting his wife, Mary, in the book *Life Politics,* which he dedicates to Mary. I was left with the strong impression that only their son had forged a stronger bond between them than their commitment to public service (Mary was a nurse dedicated to working for the National Health Service).

However, I was also aware that Ivor's work might be *misread*, even in ways that contradict each other (as overly deterministic, for example, or as relativist and uncritically postmodern, or too liberally humanist and so on). Ivor took Barry Troyna to task for just this:

> (I)n some ways you want it both ways there. Which is that you're saying that you want us to get at this sense of otherness and that it hasn't come out yet, and then you are turning around and telling me that I'm strengthening their sense of otherness. (cited in Sikes, 2011, pp. 27–28)

In some respects this kind of misreading is understandable. Although I most readily detect a social constructionist perspective in his work, Ivor works in complex and nuanced, interdisciplinary ways and is respectful of other scholarly genres and traditions; he rarely dismisses them out of hand and seeks instead to understand how and where they connect and how each might support the other, which is not to say he shies away from intellectual dispute. As Andy Hargreaves (1994) has pointed out, Ivor's "intellectual style" does not "easily wince at criticism, in jest or in earnest either in the giving or in the receipt" (p. 1). Nevertheless, part of the purpose of this book is to leave no room for doubt that Ivor's focus has always been to set "stories of action within theories of context," a phrase that he has borrowed from Lawrence Stenhouse (1975) and that he uses often.

This brings me now to the first and most important reason for our meeting, which addressed the possibility of providing a "deeper, yet accessible conceptual framework in which to negotiate and expand" understanding of his work. Could this be done? The fact that this book is now in production clearly demonstrates that we thought it could. However, in line with the need to bring some aspects of his work into sharper focus, I am presenting readers not with a framework but with a conceptual lens, produced from what I have taken to be the foundational and constitutional elements of Ivor's scholarship. This is not a matter of semantics alone. The main advantage of a lens over a framework is that it cannot easily be reassembled or reconfigured or tinkered with in some other way, at least not without fundamentally changing its constitution. Even if it is made dull it can be reground and repolished.

I have still taken equally seriously the requirements of interpretive depth and accessibility. The latter task is made less challenging by the fact that, first, Ivor has written much in very accessible ways (interviews, stories, biographical and autobiographical material). Second, the motivation for his prolific output is to act as scribe for the community from which he comes, and for other similar communities. This is not to say that Ivor thinks only some people can speak for themselves. On the contrary, he has repeatedly expressed his love of and respect for oral traditions and has strongly linked such traditions with the community, particularly the family, into which he was born. He has emphasized that oral expressions are in no way innately inferior to written forms of expression. His grandfather Jim could not read or write, and yet he left an enduring legacy as a storyteller, for example. My view is that anyone who has read Ivor's work and would still argue otherwise is out to make mischief.

But oral storytelling communities are disadvantaged, particularly in societies where the written word holds sway, their stories and histories more vulnerable to extinction. Thus acting as a scribe is not a matter of putting words into someone's mouth, but of recording words uttered. The scribe is merely an instrument for converting words into a form that cannot be lost to time, or be redefined by more powerful constituencies, at least not as easily. To be a scribe is therefore to perform a service. Being of service is fundamental to the concept of the public intellectual and this in turn is fundamental to understanding Ivor's life and work.

There is a third aspect to Ivor's accessibility. Andrew Sayer (2011) has argued convincingly that sociologists too readily dismiss the idea that there are things about which people care very much, real things about which it is entirely understandable to care, where not caring would be incomprehensible. He maintains that accounting for this in terms of socialization and other sociological concepts is reductive and dehumanizing. Ivor's intellectual project and his work connect with Sayer's argument. At its heart is the conviction that people do care about things, that we do theorize about our own lives, and that these lay theories and practical reasonings do count, albeit in ways that also need to be interrogated and contextualized. So his writing makes sense because it connects with life events and with feelings about them. In support of this contention I will give the example of my own decision to leave teaching.

I got my first job teaching German and French in a comprehensive school in 1983. I had become a teacher for many reasons, some selfish, some pragmatic, some idealistic, and not least because it made my parents proud of me. But I had joined the profession in turbulent times and over the years I became more and more dissatisfied with the changes being driven through, which I thought reduced the meaning and purpose of education to something that could be checked against a list of skills and competencies. What is more, I did take in a personal way some of the anti-teacher rhetoric that was being employed to garner public support for ideologically motivated change (that would nevertheless have such far-reaching and real consequences for the majority of the nation's children). How could I not? When I left teaching and went to work, for rather more money, in the financial services industry my mother was still not to be persuaded I had made the right move. "But Yvonne. You were a teacher!" she cried, paying little heed to the fact that public respect for teachers was no longer something that could be taken for granted. Having two children also brought many changes to my personal and professional life, but the tipping point was the prospect of the National Curriculum. The passage of time has dulled my recollection of my specific objections to it but I do recall lamenting, "We may as well just give them a phrase book and tell them to learn that."

So I finally made a decision to leave teaching in 1995. I last set foot in a comprehensive classroom in 2002 and I am still teaching now, albeit very little and in a university rather than a comprehensive school. This signals, I think, how conflicted I was about my decision. Reading Ivor's work, which recognizes the centrality of teachers to curriculum reform, helped me to appreciate the interplay of what I was doing and feeling—lesson after lesson, day after day, term after term, and year after year—and what was happening on the broader stage. I wish I had read it at the time. It would have saved me a lot of heartache and soul searching. Despite the obvious implication of political interventions in education in my decision to go, and relieved as I was to be out of it, leaving the profession felt more like desertion, dereliction of duty, and personal failure rather than a response to those interventions.

The book, as the title indicates, is organized into two broad sections. The first section, "Reading Ivor Goodson," starts by outlining the fundamental and constitutional elements of the conceptual lens, and these will be gathered under three organizing principles: "holding on," "the public intellectual," and "stories of action in theories of context." The interplay of the personal and the political sits at the heart of all three, but has a different inflection for each. Holding on focuses on the role of continuity and consistency in Ivor as a person and in his life and work and why it is apposite to use the expression *life/work* in this connection. The public intellectual sets out what Ivor himself has said about what it means to be a public intellectual and why it is unwise to proceed with your own intellectual projects without due consideration of the way external influences, particularly but not exclusively political forces, can position and reposition the meaning of what you are about. Stories of action in theories of context traces the contours of Ivor's commitment to projects of social justice, locating it in the social and historical conditions of his own biography: his background, his training as a historian and career as a teacher, and his subsequent return to academe.

A bridging chapter, "Life Politics," marks the transition from the development of the conceptual lens and its deployment in a reading of his substantive contribution. We will then move in largely chronological order from the publication of *School Subjects and Curriculum Change* in 1983 to his most recent publications in the field of narrative. These chapters are headed "Curriculum," "Teachers' Lives and Professional Knowledge," and "Narrative," but, in view of the sheer volume of his publications, they cannot take the form of a detailed or even a brief explication of each of his works. I do focus on some key tests, but in the main *reading* here is to be taken in the meta sense of coming to the overarching and underlying ideas and motivations they reflect.

Although my approach is chronological, I have not been concerned to sequence my narrative. Each chapter is intended to stand in its own corner, but there are three broad reasons for taking a chronological approach nonetheless. The first arises out of Ivor's conviction that covering topics chronologically pays due regard to the importance of historical context. In other words, ordering the material in this way is consistent with the importance of historical and social context, a mainstay of Ivor's conceptualization of the life history approach. Thus, the changing political scene in the UK produced a substantive shift in focus in his work at the start of the 1990s. The second is that it makes explicit Ivor's "intellectual journey" and states the importance of the personal significance of events in the evolution of his thinking and the focus of his interests: the fact he did not learn to read until he was 8, his leaving school at the age of 15 and subsequent return to education after the intervention of a teacher, breaking off an academic career teaching undergraduate history to become a teacher in comprehensive schools, his efforts to teach things that engaged his pupils, his return to the academy, leaving the UK to work in Canada and the US before returning to the UK, to what was clearly the immense relief of his wife and son. All these events have been personally significant but have also affected his scholarly concerns.

A third advantage of the chronological approach is that it obviates the need to group topics thematically (the headings I have used are more in the way of umbrella terms). I will expand on this statement in the next chapter, but in short, a chronological approach releases the material to a greater extent from the influence of my organizing principles and allows the underlying and overarching raison d'être for Ivor's unrelenting work rate and his total commitment to social justice to do most of the talking.

The second section is titled "Teaching Ivor Goodson." If the first section broadly focuses on substance, the second broadly focuses on methodology, although the way in which each has informed the other will be emphasized, because as William Pinar (1995) points out:

> Goodson's historical focus is unique, informed by life history and politics. His interest in life history is informed by politics and history. And his political theory is embedded in history and life history. (p. xxi)

The consistency, coherence, and harmony of Ivor's ideas are an essential aspect of the conceptual lens that is being applied. The borders between the private individual and the public intellectual are nebulous. Indeed, Ivor's tireless intellectual and academic endeavors can be seen as a means of actualizing many of his private hopes, dreams, and desires. He also works in a modality of "holding on" not only to the formative experiences of his own childhood but to a longer family history of "independent thinking" (2005a). He emphasizes to Jess Moriarty (2012) that he does "applied writing," linked to "probably the overarching concern, which is with social justice generally and that goes back to my background." This section therefore takes as its starting point a conversation I had with Ivor as "Reading Ivor Goodson" neared completion. After trying a number of approaches, this best addressed the challenge of not creating false divisions between substance and methodology and between the different aspects of his life/work. What is more, a central tenet, if not *the* central tenet, of Ivor's approach to pedagogy is that teaching and learning is an interactive enterprise. He regards "dialogic en-

counters" such as conversations and interviews also as "pedagogic encounters" and a conversation performs each of these imperatives of his thinking.

In the introduction to a volume of his collected works (2005a), Ivor also
writes that one never knows which lines of thought will become fruitful and
which turn out to be a cul-de-sac. There is a tension therefore between this
sense of organic development and the necessary reviewing, abridging, and
appraisal that had to go on in this volume. With this in mind I have been at
pains to avoid bringing a sense of closure and completeness to the reading of
his work or to reduce it to a bland and indifferent account from which all
passion is absent and which is at odds with the vibrancy of the originals. In
other words, I have tried, despite all the cherry-picking and summarizing and
sound-biting, to retain the "Ivor-ness" of what I have written about. This
book is about a morally inflected approach to scholarship, one dedicated to a
politics of transformation, driven by a practical, passionate, principled humanity. The proposition that Ivor Goodson is concerned with lived realities
and the processes of their production and that his theories articulate that
which is common sense to those who live them on a daily basis sits at the
heart of the continuing relevance of his work, not just to academics, students,
and those in or entering the teaching profession, but also to anyone with an
interest in a more just society.

Section 1. Reading Ivor Goodson

Chapter 1

Preamble

I am still interested in inclusive ways of being a social man.

(Goodson, 2011, p. 1)

The overarching purpose of the chapters that constitute "Reading Ivor Goodson" is to provide an opportunity for readers old and new to acquaint themselves with the meaning of the term *life/work*. I will be using this term to express the coherence between Ivor's life politics and his work as a public intellectual and to foreground the integrity of the way in which he carries out his mission to serve his tribe and other tribes who are similarly positioned through his scholarship. Spending some time with Ivor's ideas, his scholarship, and his published work furnishes an interpretive lens through which deeper insights and fresh perspectives may be gained. My initial concern was that this might be a redundant rather than a necessary undertaking, but on the contrary, despite the fact that Ivor has been consistent and unambiguous about his purpose and the underlying motivations for the work he does, the message has not always come through, or it has been misheard or ignored. Ragna Adlandsvik (Goodson, 2011) articulates the task before me when she states how important it is to keep explaining Ivor's position because his arguments have not yet been understood or have been misinterpreted.

Finding a way to do this is no small matter. As a teacher and even before he formally entered academe, Ivor was writing about education. The weight and volume of his published work is immense, and not all of it has been published. He still writes every day and even writes in his sleep and has ideas waiting to be set down on paper in the morning. His scholarship describes a vast and varied landscape and has transcended the borders of mainstream scholarship, both figuratively and literally. It is rare for UK scholars to cross national borders or to have the geographical reach that Ivor does. He has deliberately made a point of being a "traveling organic intellectual" (2011, p. xi). Hence his work is known in

Brazil and in Spanish-speaking countries of South America, in China, across Europe and Scandinavia, and in Indonesia, Japan, and Malaysia. It has been translated into several languages. Wherever he has traveled he has formed alliances and has collaborated with distinguished and respected scholars, too innumerable to mention individually here but who can be located in the coauthorship of many publications.

Substantively, his attention has been claimed by a seemingly disparate array of topics: the social histories of school subjects and the curriculum; theories of curriculum that include an appreciation of continuities as well as ruptures; pedagogical theory; narrative theory and the narrative construction of lives; narrative learning; education policy, particularly that pertaining to change and reforms; historiography and the work of the Annaliste school and how that maps onto the study of change and reform; professional lives, particularly of public professionals and specifically but not exclusively of teachers, professional knowledge, and identities; an overarching concern with life projects and what he has termed *life politics*; second-generation return migration and computers in classrooms. His ideas are paradigm-defying and in terms of methodology his contribution to the rehabilitation of life history approaches and their application to the study of education is inestimable.

In the process of grappling with the task of making all this accessible without resorting to sound bites or a whistle stop tour, my ideas coalesced around three general approaches. The first is encapsulated in the metaphor of the *framework* and involved delineating certain parameters within which to consider his work. This approach has the advantage of creating a well-defined space in which to do this. However, it also seemed likely that trying to accommodate the work within the constraints of a single framework would hardly be conducive to doing justice to its range and depth, particularly as this relatively slim volume has already imposed its own limits. It is one thing to make the work accessible within necessary confines. It is quite another to reduce or attenuate it, particularly as the magnitude of his accomplishments reflects the passion and commitment to his mission that must be at the heart of any interpretation of what he does. Frameworks might provide a helpful structure but they can be too rigid on the one hand and impermanent and vulnerable to reassembly and reconfiguration on the other.

The second approach involves locating the themes running through his scholarship, tracing their trajectory through the vast and varied landscape of his written output and bringing them into sharper focus, thus avoiding issues of contraction and diminution. However, putting this approach into practice reveals three issues. First, these themes are already visible to the naked eye and therefore locating them is a redundant activity. To reiterate, Ivor is unwaveringly explicit about the origins, foundations, and motivations of his scholarship. He sets out his intentions and the underlying principles of his work with great clarity and consistency and in some detail. Some of this detail is found in places that might be overlooked—prefaces, forewords, and introductions to his works and his website, for example—but he has also dedicated entire chapters and papers to the purpose of explaining himself. *Learning, Curriculum, Life Politics* (2005a), for example, can be seen as his attempt to do just this and to house the important themes of his scholarship under one roof.

Moreover, in preparation for writing this book, when I was reading chronologically through his work, I concluded that there was in effect only one thread running through it and indeed through the whole of his life project. He has tirelessly worked to realize his mission for a just society and in this sense he is carrying forward the Goodson family motto ("We're a very persistent family"). He realized early that this would entail grappling with the dynamics of power between individuals and their location on the broader sociopolitical canvas. He is also wise to the way in which broader sociopolitical and cultural conditions serve to inform our daily lives, to provide the scripted resources for the stories we tell about ourselves and our lives and to "re-position," or change the significance of what we are doing. He has therefore stayed alert to movements on the broader stage to anticipate and respond preemptively. He has been prepared to relocate his concerns to where they are being contested at any given time and it is this rather than concerns about his academic standing that has driven his career. Regardless of where this has taken him, his underlying concerns and commitments have nonetheless stayed constant. For all these reasons, configuring his intellectual endeavors as discrete activities that are divorced from the rest of his life is simply a doomed project.

A trenchant example here is Ivor's decision, after many years of intense involvement with it, to shift his attention away from the study of curriculum. He explains that his work on curriculum and pedagogy was situated in the historical context of the 1970s when social inclusion was being pursued through the development of comprehensive schools, whether that was for economic or ideological reasons. As a public intellectual he therefore saw research on curriculum and pedagogy as a contribution to the aims of social democratic government. However, in the 1980s those sociopolitical aims had changed and the struggle over curriculum was overshadowed by a market struggle for position and resources. Curriculum was no longer a major site of contestation and curriculum studies were increasingly attending to matters of implementation. Ivor therefore turned his attention more to the study of teachers' lives and to how professional knowledge was being (re)configured, to the exploration of people's life missions and moral purpose, and the way those interact with broader social and political missions. Redirecting his gaze did not signify that Ivor no longer had an interest in curriculum but that his role as a public intellectual required him to respond to the changing macroeconomic, sociopolitical climate.

The third approach involves the provision of a particular kind of conceptual *lens*. This is the approach I am taking here not least because a lens can be put to work in a number of different ways. It can be used to scrutinize detail or to take in the whole view and it can also serve as a prism through which to consider his ideas. Accessing Ivor's life/work through this lens, we see that it has sprung from ideas formed in childhood, which is in turn, or at least in part, attributable to his growing up at a time when there was a desire for a more just society. The origins of his concerns can also be traced back to his being born into a particular family, one that drew on traditions of independent thinking and oral cultures and into a class that has continued to be disadvantaged. Here "disadvantaged" operates not as an adjective or a descriptor suggestive of passive acceptance and of victim status, but as a verb, indicating that actual work and powerful forces are involved in bringing it about. In other words, people of this class are not powerless victims, but there are powerful mechanisms that are engaged to exclude them socially, politically, and culturally to which they have no choice but to respond in whatever way. Working at this interface is foundational to his scholarship as he makes visible and offers strategies for destabilizing this dynamic— whether through curriculum form, through pedagogy, or through reclaiming narrative control.

Above all, using the metaphor of the lens makes misrepresentation of his work more difficult. It is fair to say that Ivor does not balk at criticisms of his work. It is obvious from some of the exchanges he has had with other scholars that he enjoys the spirited argument and the reiteration of his intellectual project. He welcomes the opportunity to set out why certain things mean a great deal to him. He is passionately attached to the ends of his scholarship, to inclusivity and social justice, but embraces arguments about the different means by which this might be achieved. Above all he is clear that:

> there are by and large people out there who do not want the disadvantaged to succeed, they do not want vernacular voices to be heard, they do not want the kids in the rock 'n' roll band to make it and they invent all sorts of reasons for that but basically they don't want that to happen. (quoted in Moriarty, 2012, p.25)

It is against these people that he has been determined to stand.

Conceiving a particular interpretive device and setting out its advantages is one thing. There still remains the task of deciding how it is to be constituted. In this case the decision was facilitated by the fact that there are certain characteristics of his scholarship to which Ivor often refers: "holding on," "the public intellectual," and "stories of action in theories of context." It is these that I have taken to be the constitutive elements of the conceptual lens through which the substantive foci of this section might be read. I therefore begin this section by setting out what is meant by each. I then present an overview of the overarching concept of "life politics," which I argue acts as a repository for the constancy of his concerns, before proceeding to three sites where he explored them: curriculum, teachers' lives, and narrative. The leitmotif throughout is that Ivor has lived out his social project, or his mission as he defines it, attending in a number of ways to a nexus of concerns and preoccupations and always articulating his response to these consistently and unequivocally.

Chapter 2

Holding On

I have never thought there would have been another way to live my life in terms of my original loyalties. That doesn't mean that I am bigoted about more privileged groups—I am happy to interact with other groups, but my questions always are when these new initiatives come in: How will they work with the groups of people who are my people, my tribe? What does it mean for my tribe? I guess I love the people I came from. I have never met better people. So, I should speak for them.

(Goodson, 2011, p. 3)

It is no exaggeration to say that the concept of holding on is synonymous with Ivor's modus operandi. In his own words, he works in a "modality of holding on." In one respect this is a fairly straightforward concept articulating the way in which certain beliefs and values, formed early in his life, have continued to inform and shape his scholarly concerns. They inform his theoretical perspectives and intellectual and hence life projects to the extent that we might conceive of this as life/work, and they guide (or even direct) their orientation. "Holding on," like so much in Ivor's scholarship, is therefore an artless expression of an intricate and powerful idea.

At first glance the notion of holding on seems to contradict another central tenet of his scholarship, that is, the phenomenon of "repositioning," whereby the influence of forces that reside and operate on the macro level changes the *meaning* of actions on the micro level, even when the action itself stays constant. But "holding on" on the one hand and being responsive to the changing contexts in which we are located on the other are far from being contradictory. Nowhere is this more powerfully illustrated than in Ivor's insistence that we hold on to history and to an understanding of its pendulum swings, its waves and its circularity, in order to understand the present but also in preparation for the future. This offers the possibility of resisting the debilitating effects of, for example, narratives about the "end of history." In other words, holding on is not synonymous with "carrying on the same way regardless" but its opposite. Indeed it is imperative to anticipate changes that lie ahead and to work out a strategic response to the forces that prevail at the particular junctures in which we are located, whether these are for good or ill. It is in this respect that Ivor has been particularly effective.

An example from "The Educational Researcher as Public Intellectual" (Goodson, 1999) serves as an example in support of this contention. After World War II educational policy in the UK and the US reflected the fact that powerful forces were committed to egalitarian projects. Educational researchers who also embraced this commitment therefore played a vital role and occupied a central position in wider political contexts. This is no longer the case, because far from pursuing egalitarian goals, global forces are effecting the (re)stratification of social life. Pursuing egalitarian goals is thus no longer relevant. It is at best marginal in this macro-political context at this particular historical juncture. Holding on to a historical perspective addresses the necessity of tailoring our actions and responses to the conditions of our existence while at the same time not sacrificing dearly held principles and values.

The case for understanding the idea of holding on, its origins and how it manifests in his work, is therefore compelling, but attempting to achieve this through a conceptual unpacking or unpicking requires a mammoth effort and actually serves to undermine its force and significance. A better approach is to ask what it is that Ivor is holding on to, and this is what I will now do.

Independence

Ivor is not interested in fitting in or becoming part of the establishment or the mainstream. As Joe Kincheloe (1997) diplomatically puts it, "Ivor sees the universe from an angle that never fails to inform and entertain" (p. ix). Before the introduction, albeit patchy and imperfect, of the comprehensive system in England, most working-class children who got a place at grammar school tried to "fit in" and absorbed, or at least wore, the values of the "hidden curriculum" of those schools. This does not apply to Ivor. He refused to leave his original loyalties behind and left school at 15 to work in a crisp factory. This tradition of independence is also true of his scholarly and pedagogic activities. His commitment is to the flow of power from the margin to the center.

Independent thinking can be both liberating and exclusionary, and Ivor is aware of both its possibilities and its restrictions. Nevertheless, he positions his independence less as an informed choice and more as a familial legacy and part of his birthright. Ivor grew up in a village near Reading and he researched some of its history, discovering that in the eighteenth century the local landlord began to enclose the land to buy the cottages on it, but his mother's family had resisted by relocating outside the enclosure:

> Most labourers in the village accepted the dispossession involved: That my own family chose to resist this economic order by locating in Cobblers City speaks of an enduring independence of spirit. This spirit hopefully informs my own chosen vocation and my pedagogic moments. . . . Patterns of dispossession and displacement it seems endure. As to independent responses, well, we shall see. (Goodson, 2005a, p. 15)

Almost everything he does illustrates and supports the enduring legacy of independent thinking and action to which he refers above, but the following examples stand out: he went to university in the 1960s in Teddy Boy garb; he retained an interest in popular culture rather than cultivating an interest in the "highbrow" and, as a teacher, his flat would be full of pupils rifling through his record collection and playing music on his stereo (Walker, 1973); he gave up a post lecturing in history to go and teach in a comprehensive school; when he got funding to research the introduction of computers in Canadian schools, he proceeded to question the fundamental rationale of this policy; when policymakers were demanding "large scale, quantitative information" (Blunkett, 2000, p. 20) he became yet more interested in stories, in narrative pedagogies, in theories about how and why we narrate our lives in the way we do, and in coming to a theory of narrative.

All of this might be interpreted as the desire to be "trendy" (Goodson, 1997a). It is important, however, to recognize how labeling is used as a mechanism of oppression. It is no easy matter to swim against the tide or go against the grain or to stand in opposition to powerful forces. Ivor's use of the metaphors of combat and battle reflects I think the lived reality of doing so, rather than a preference for those metaphors above others (this was for me a striking aspect of his first published book, *School Subjects and Curriculum Change* [1983]). But the minute the struggle is relabeled as "trendy" it is minimized, trivialized, reconfigured, individualized, and thus marginalized, and the alternative or dissenting voice is silenced or ridiculed.

Ivor has addressed the way in which the important work of theorizing can be undermined in this way (1997a). He has also surfaced how dominant forces must sometimes strive long and hard to win (1989). The following oversimplified but nevertheless pertinent example of the reversal of curriculum reform begun in the 1960s in the UK serves to give a flavor of the protracted processes and considerable efforts that are sometimes entailed. It involved provoking what amounted to a moral panic that started with the publication of the first two of five *Black Papers* (Cox & Dyson, 1969a, 1969b). Jim Callaghan's (1976) Ruskin College speech was also a significant landmark. Although Callaghan requested that the response to his speech be positive rather than defensive, the very act of speaking escalated fears about how and what children were being taught in schools. A report by Her Majesty's Inspectorate about teacher quality (HMI, 1983) might then be seen as marking the zenith (or nadir) of this moral panic and the tipping point for change.

To return to the matter of independence, therefore, it is an impulse and an imperative rather than something to be chosen and worn lightly, but it must not be mistaken for a desire to remain isolated. On the contrary, Ivor emphasizes and has demonstrated that he is a social man working in inclusive ways. Therefore, even though some of his most recent work is concerned with developing narrative theory, he still posits it as "a drive to stay close to ordinary working life culture and not become entirely detached within university academia" (2013, p. 4). In his research he emphasizes a collaborative approach and equable relationship, what he calls a "fair trade," between researcher and participant. Independence also means that he remains determined not to research things as they are, but as they might be if we were working toward a fair and just society that included groups such as those from whence he comes.

History

I touched on the importance of holding on to history in the opening paragraphs to this chapter, but I want now to flesh this out. When Ivor left school at 15 he had one qualification—in history. He studied history as an undergraduate and on graduating became a lecturer in history and began doctoral research on Irish immigrants in Victorian England. Thus both his inclination and his formative academic experiences ensure that the importance of historical perspectives is embedded in his scholarship.

Trying to subtract the importance of a historical perspective from Ivor's work is a doomed enterprise, so entangled is it with every other aspect of his scholarship.

As far as Ivor is concerned, it is not a matter of "raiding history," that is, of using historical evidence to "prove a contemporary point" (1984, p. 26). The reason he holds on to this sense of history is not explained either by his personal leanings or his early career. He argues for the inclusion of history in part because it has the ability to transform research agendas through the provision of fresh and alternative perspectives and the addition of new questions to be explored. In part it is also because omitting it can lead to a failure of analysis.

At the end of the 1980s Ivor was critical of the fact that ahistorical analyses were failing on four counts. First, they were missing the way in which the "new" National Curriculum in the UK was actually reestablishing older forms conceived in 1904, forms in which subjects had primacy. In other words, "historical amnesia" was permitting "curriculum reconstruction to be presented as curriculum revolution" (1989, p. 137). Second, this also meant that analysis was not picking up the fact that this incarnation of curriculum had produced the reform initiatives of the 1960s and 1970s. To put it simply, there was little effective resistance among those who should have been exercising it, leaving the way free for a return to what had already proved itself lacking. Thirdly, there was a concomitant failure to acknowledge that curriculum study was grounded in the "revolutionary" ideas that underpinned these initiatives and excluded a focus on continuities and how curriculum can be reproduced as well as transformed (1984).

However, it is the fourth failure of analysis that disturbs Ivor the most. Were the omission of history simply a failure of scholarship it would be bad enough. Unfortunately, though, failure to give due regard to history results most often in amnesia, and the consequences of this reverberate in the lived and material realities of those people to whom Ivor has remained attached. Rolling back the clock to a subject-based curriculum serves as a mechanism of exclusion for these groups, a theme I will revisit when we focus more closely on Ivor's work on curriculum, particularly curriculum theory.

Optimism

This last point has perhaps introduced a note of pessimism into a consideration of his work. This is misleading because taking a historical view of events has often imbued Ivor's writing with a sense of optimism. He states, for example, that:

> Public knowledge and public education have historically been subject to recurrent pendulum swings between the emancipatory/enlightenment vision and the darker forces of subordination and social control. (1999, p. 278)

He is also persuaded that curriculum will again become a major site of contestation and possibility. He therefore declares that he can be optimistic even when there is little reason to be so and even when there is no sound evidential basis to support the wisdom of taking such a stance. But it is important to understand that optimism here is not simply the manifestation of a sunny disposition, although he most definitely has this, too, but can be seen as a moral stance (Issa & Pick, 2010).

That said, his optimism that the contribution he and others have striven to make in realizing a more just and inclusive society will eventually bear fruit has taken a bruising of late, due in no small measure to the way in which he sees society become increasingly stratified and the possibility of a just society correspondingly receding. He has cause for concern because, as I outlined earlier, he knows that this is not happening by chance and that there are, at least, three powerful forces at work that need to be factored into an analysis of the times.

First, the phenomenon of globalization, far from having a unifying influence and serving to blur boundaries, has created divisions that were they uniform in macro and micro contexts would be bad enough. But, I once heard Slavoj Žižek (2008) say, simply but with great insight, that the trouble with globalization is that it is not global enough. Rather than benefits being available to all and the burdens of privation being evenly distributed, benefits and burdens cluster together as separate entities, serve as markers of difference, consolidate privilege, and exacerbate deprivation. Put simply, to those that have shall be given, and given exponentially, so that the gap between those who already had political power, narrative control, wealth, security, access to information, and so on and those who did not has widened at a frightening pace.

Second, and illustrative of how the power of local influences is still germane despite globalization, local market forces can also result in the stratification of space, so that, for example, a certain type of school will be located in the suburbs and another in the inner city. This is disheartening to Ivor because he holds that "once that space is stratified it's very hard to break that old struggle to hold privileges" (2011, p. 58).

A third force is that of technology and its role in the stratification of information, accomplished in terms of its associated hardware and software and also in terms of who controls the construction of "cyberspace" (Goodson, Knobel, Lankshear, & Mangan, 2002). On a simple level, if only certain people can afford this hardware (and bear in mind that there is a relentless impetus to continually upgrade it), it follows that only these privileged groups will have access to information. Less privileged groups will not. The implications of this are many and far-reaching but as a start Ivor sees that it requires thinking about how "cyberspace" is being constructed as a particular kind of social space, an exclusionary rather than an inclusive one.

In addition to the injurious effects of stratification, Ivor is concerned about the way in which powerful, often global, elites seem to have seized narrative control. This means, for example, that the failure of bankers and of governments to respond appropriately to the financial crisis can be represented as attributable to overspending on public services (2011). It also means that the top 0.01% of the world's wealthiest people can peddle "The Big Lie" (Krugman, 2012) that allows them to amass even greater wealth at the expense of the majority, including the world's very poorest people.

And yet, and this is where we can clearly discern its moral force, Ivor ultimately reasserts his optimism through a belief that the currently "silent majority" is fighting back, although he contends that the absence of a thoroughgoing theory of evil may be hampering an effective response. Again he relies on the importance of a historical perspective:

> As always in social change we have to pick ourselves up and begin again. This time a little wiser, less believing in governmental and global good intentions, and more cognisant of the need for "theories of evil" as we pursue our purposes. (Goodson, 1999, p. 287)

Chapter 3

The Public Intellectual

When public services are being reconceptualised and reconstructed in helpful and broadly supportive ways by sympathetic politicians, the educational researcher as public intellectual emerges from the shadows.

(Goodson, 1999, p. 281)

Although it is a seemingly simple and straightforward term, the expression *public intellectual* resonates with the dynamics of what amounts to Ivor's mission. To understand what this term embodies is therefore to understand what he has been about for all these years. A core and pivotal concept in reading Ivor Goodson, it might also be understood as the touchstone and lynchpin of his work and the lodestar of his life. Ivor allies it to Gramsci's idea of the "organic intellectual." Its meaning has developed over the years, assuming various incarnations and being enacted in different ways. He also augments the concept to include the idea of traveling, of coming to understanding in the context of globalization and the revolution in communication wrought by digital technologies. It is therefore quite a task to summarize what it means and it makes more sense not to treat what follows as a definitive statement, although it does serve as a prismatic lens through which to read later chapters.

Underpinning the idea and the work of the public intellectual is a commitment to public service, evidenced by the many years of research Ivor has carried out with people who work in that sector and by his early concern with curriculum research. But this is only a reflection of a broader and more profound commitment to public life that pervades every aspect of his life as a whole. In this sense, being a public intellectual epitomizes the dynamic between the personal and the political. For example, when he talks about meeting his wife Mary, who was a nurse in the National Health Service (NHS), he emphasizes how they were "engaged in the same social project" and that they "have stayed the same way all the way through" (2011, p. 1). It is therefore axiomatic to read Ivor's work as a wholly integrated manifestation of the man himself.

However, the meaning of public service is vulnerable to reinterpretation. Changes to the NHS also mean that the work of nurses has been repositioned (and having friends who have been nursing for more than 30 years I hear this often). Moreover, "(a)s the public sphere comes under attack the very relevance of applied research and public intellectual discussion is itself challenged" (Goodson, 2011, p. ix). Much of this is allied to the reconfiguration of what "public" signifies in light of the forces of globalization. It is therefore worth taking some time to consider the "public" aspect of public intellectual even though some of the force of the whole will inevitably be lost in the process.

On Ivor's terms the notion of public is closely allied to the idea of an open and inclusive space. It is ironic that the phenomenon of globalization serves also to make spaces more exclusive and Ivor worries about their fragmentation, stratification, and privatization (2007). Although he also mentions other examples such as the privatization of space in shopping malls in the US where it is now illegal to hold public protests (1999), he is most concerned when this is enacted within the sphere of education through, predominantly but not exclusively, the involvement of corporate interests.

It has always been the case that different kinds of schools existed in different kinds of places. It is also the case that the processes of stratification are many and varied. For example, the establishment of comprehensive schools in the UK, far from providing a new model for inclusive education, served more to internalize distinction. What happened was not so much a change of system but a change of location, with the same divisions housed under one roof instead of in separate buildings. What makes the current privatization of education an even more pressing concern is its imperative for a return on investment, which looks likely to reinforce and compound such processes. A system pervaded by the tensions between profit maximization and corporate social responsibility cannot but produce a redefinition of the meaning and purpose of education. When "markets respect the rich and powerful at the expense of the poor" (Goodson, 2011, p. 111) the notion of public education as a vehicle for equal opportunities and for social justice is undermined. As a result of the changing shape of public spheres, the work and the role of the public intellectual becomes reinterpreted and repositioned (1999). Thus public intellectuals must redefine their task. To put it in simplistic terms, fighting against a mercantile conceptualization and realization of education may, for now, be more pressing than realizing the goals of inclusivity themselves, although the two are closely allied.

The reconfiguration of the public space thus has ramifications for intellectual work. Perhaps the most important task is for public intellectuals to acknowledge that their work is vulnerable to this "crisis of positionality" in the first place, that the meaning of what they do might change, even if they continue to do the same thing. Public intellectuals must therefore not only be responsive but proactive and strategic, insights that Ivor has adapted from the work of Wini Breines (1980). In "The Educational Researcher as a Public Intellectual" (1999), Ivor illustrates this contention by critiquing the emphasis in educational research on "practice," divorced from an equal theoretical contribution. He sees this as amounting to an endorsement of a concept of teaching as delivery and implementation and hence of a view of "education" that does not include, let alone serve, the very groups he seeks to represent.

This does not mean abandoning a commitment to "stand on behalf of those who do not speak, in favor of them, and to try and develop cognitive maps of power for those groups" (Goodson, 2011, p. 3). Indeed, in the context of powerful macro-political forces, the requirement to represent "groups who in some ways do not know how it operates and in some ways get a worse deal" (2011, p. 3) is even more of an imperative. In Ivor's view it takes on the hue of a "moral career." Part of this must be to make visible the changing ways in which public issues become private troubles:

> What is required in reforms around the western world is some pause in the frenetic pace of restructuring to reflect on the profound dangers that emerge when the dedicated and dutiful groups that underpin our public services begin to voice their alienation and despair in growing numbers. (2007, p. 147)

I will return to look in more detail at Ivor's promotion of the life history approach as a way to accomplish this in later chapters. But it is important not only to see this in methodological terms but as an expression of the beliefs that sit at the heart of his public intellectual work.

Theoretical perspective is a vital contribution to debates by the public intellectual, furnishing theories of context to stories of action. This is a central tenet of Ivor's work, which I will explore more fully in the next chapter. However, before I do, I want to spend some time with the notion of public engagement. I see this as a different idea altogether from that of the public intellectual. I must emphasize that, although Ivor has also used the term "public engagement," the distinction is mine. However, when he states that "the term public intellectual is itself (besides sounding somewhat pious!) subject to considerable contestation at the moment" (2011, p. ix), I would argue that some of those contested meanings inhere in *public engagement*.

I would venture to say that *public engagement* can no longer be used as a neutral term or a broad-based idiom signifying involvement with wider constituencies outside those of the academy. It has a particular currency and a particular contemporary inflection, not only in academic circles. Its meaning has become so incompatible with the kind of public intellectualism that Ivor advocates that it is antithetical to it. In other words, *public engagement* is tethered to a model of involvement that Ivor has clearly and consistently criticized. So before going any further I want to spend some time with *public engagement* in order to bring *public intellectualism* into even sharper relief.

Public Engagement, Research Impact, and Value for Money

The idea of public engagement within the realm of the academy is informed, predominantly but not exclusively, by debates about the purpose of academic institutions, of academics and of higher education. Although the term *public engagement* has the potential to articulate any number of different positions within these debates, it has become associated with the idea that investment in academic institutions, in higher education and its associated activities (teaching, learning, pedagogy, research, knowledge generation, and so on) should represent value for money. To my mind it is not the concept of "value for money" itself that causes problems. I do not believe I am deluding myself when I say that few among us are happy to contemplate deliberately wasting money. Tensions arise, however, when it comes to considering what constitutes "value."

Without becoming embroiled in economic debates, the dominant understanding of value in terms of the purpose of academic institutions and higher education is now entangled in the imperative to deliver *direct, immediate, visible,* and *measurable* returns on investments made. The services that can be provided by academics to constituencies outside the academy are seen as the principle way in which to achieve these returns. Therefore these services are engaged to improve, streamline, and make more efficient that which already is, rather than to challenge, undermine, or change systems or processes or to go beyond the "state of the art." And they are far removed from those designed to create a climate for imagining the possibility of change.

In support of this contention I would point to the particular ways in which research impact is now being construed. Again, I would say that this idea is not problematic in itself. Without impact of some description, academic labor would amount to little more than busywork. The problems arise, I contend, because of the specific, restrictive, and emaciated meaning of impact, which gains currency within the Research Excellence Framework (REF), the "system for assessing the quality of research in UK higher education institutions (HEIs)" (www.ref.ac.uk). It is in this specific meaning of impact, with its emphasis on the establishment of causal links, that the idea of public engagement has somehow become implicated. As I touched on in the previous chapter, Ivor has undertaken many projects that have engaged with "real world" issues. His long involvement in research into many public sector services (education, obviously, but also nurses and the medical profession, social services, and the police) has given him a profound understanding of its "ecology" (Goodson, 2007). However, it may yet be difficult to "prove" what his impact has been in REF-able terms.

One of the reasons for the challenges inherent in establishing the credentials of Ivor's impact is that he has used methods that rely on a slow burn and that generate knowledge that requires thinking through and ongoing discussion of the kind of knowledge they engender. For example, *Cyber Spaces/Social Spaces* is the result of "a decade of sustained 'watching' and thinking about ICT adoption and practice in schools" (Goodson et al., 2002, p. 2). The tensions between public intellectualism and public engagement can also be discerned in the assumption that impact must have a directly identifiable beneficiary, whose testimony as to the nature of the impact is often required as evidence. But impact can be far reaching without being directly traceable to any named individuals. An interview with Eduardo Mortimer (2007), subsequently published as part of a dossier in the Brazilian journal *Educação Em Revista,* provides a powerful illustration of this assertion.

In his introduction to the dossier, Moreira (2007) tells us that Ivor's work is "valued and distributed worldwide" but when asked about the "main achievements" of his work in the area of the social history of school subjects in the interview, Ivor responds, "It's difficult to know the main achievements." Instead he tells us something of the history of his interest in it. When pressed to answer the question about achievements more directly, he offers the following:

> The achievement is to be *sitting here and talking in Brazil* and know that the *Brazilian scholars* have used this work in their own work and in the work with their *students*. And hopefully that *this will disseminate through into the knowledge of that social and political process* which will be shared with *teachers* as well. I think if that is working and the fact that these books are in seventeen languages implies that they have some relevance in most countries and *slowly the scholars in those countries are doing the work*. The point is that I'm not going to know about Brazil, you are. But you can use the methodology and the approach to bring the socio-political understandings to educational researchers and teachers in your country. And that I think is, *the achievement will be your achievement, but it's an achievement in the method as well*. (Moreira, 2007, emphasis added)

I have added the emphasis to those of Ivor's words here that show how his ambitions for his work are incompatible with the underpinning rationale of impact. There is no immediate or direct benefit, but a slow dissemination; no named beneficiaries, "just" scholars, students, and teachers. In the final sentence he disassociates himself from any personal claim to impact at all.

Ivor's "worldwide reputation" therefore does not make sense in the world of the kind of "public engagement" that I have posited, which is one reason I have spent time distinguishing between it and public intellectualism. To summarize, public engagement is overlaid with a sense of "political quietism" (Goodson, 1999, p. 294). The engagement is with "practice as defined" (1999, p. 295). Public intellectualism, on the other hand, involves "prefigurative politics." This is a term Ivor has borrowed from Breines (1980) and can be defined in the following way:

> Prefigurative politics seeks to create and sustain within the lived practice of the movement relationships and political forms that "prefigure" and embody the desired society. (quoted in Goodson, 1999, p. 292)

In other words, public intellectualism stands as a challenge to existing regimes of power. It does not engage with them. This is why it will, I think, be a difficult task to locate Ivor's substantial impact within the confines of REF-able outputs. This does not mean, however, that we must read Ivor's work as decontextualized. On the contrary, we shall in the next chapter focus on Ivor's insistence that stories of action must always be located within theories of context.

Chapter 4

Stories of Action in Theories of Context

Only new alliances between theory and practice can remake the possibility for educational research to contribute to new visions and new structures of education.

(Goodson, 1999, p. 294)

The phrase *stories of action in theories of context* is attributable to Lawrence Stenhouse (1975). Stenhouse founded the Centre for Applied Research in Education (CARE) at the University of East Anglia in 1970 and according to Ivor "in both his writing and his action . . . (he) spoke as a public intellectual" (Goodson, 1999, p. 277). I found these words moving because in Ivor's view, the term *public intellectual* is value-laden, implying a moral career. It is also a term that also owes much to Mills (1959) who called attention to the dynamic between the biographical, the social, and the historical and, in distinguishing between "private troubles" and "public issues," provided a conceptual language for articulating the relationship between the structural and the personal. The public intellectual speaks this language in that space.

It is a term therefore that simultaneously encapsulates and articulates the underlying philosophy, key ideas, and overarching rationale of Ivor's scholarship and serves as a prismatic lens through which to examine them. It thus makes visible his ideas about power and about the dynamics of the relationship between theory and practice, the individual and the collective, and stories and context. It simultaneously stands as a normative statement about the role of the intellectual, the meaning and purpose of educational research and that of other kinds of public intellectual labor, and in this sense it is also aspirational. It is shorthand for the fundamentals of Ivor's life/work.

Public intellectual is therefore a complex term and there is simply not enough space in which to thoroughly deconstruct it, which would risk undermining its integrity anyway. What I want to do instead is to call attention to some of the ideas housed within it that have appeared as leitmotifs or recurrent themes in Ivor's work over years.

Power

Although he is at pains to set out that it is not a particularly well-drawn theory, Ivor sees power as operating at three levels: macro, micro, and mezzo. It is particularly the mezzo level that interests him. Joe Kincheloe (1997) writes:

> Understanding the propensity of political students of curriculum to focus on general cultural dynamics (macro-theories) to explain educational inequality and the tendency of phenomenologically-based students to privilege the particularistic domain of classroom interaction (micro-theories), Goodson early on recognized the need to analyze the interrelation of the two spheres of activity. . . . In this manner Goodson places himself on the middle ground between the theoretical and the particular. (p. xv)

Ivor recognizes the importance of locating himself here because it is where, in Kincheloe's words, the "two way (and more) flow of power" can be best observed and analyzed. As we shall see, there is a crucial temporal element to this. To be located here is to be Janus-faced, to use Ivor's own term, to look back at its historical antecedents and forward to its potential ramifications.

Ivor explains his theory of the workings of power in an interview with Daniel Feldman and Mariano Palamidessi (Goodson, 2011):

> I read the world differently, I don't think domination works as systematic pression. I believe it works as mediated surrender by subordinate groups. That's a very different conception of power. (p. 36)

The mediation to which Ivor refers here takes place in schools and in classrooms, for example, and in setting out the importance of different loci for the study of curriculum. Ivor advocated going "through the schoolhouse door" (1994, p. 12; Goodson & Anstead, 2010) to work at the interface of the micro and the macro. It is here that the policies that have been "handed down" are mediated rather· than unflinchingly implemented where the "refraction"—that is, the processes of re-interpretation, recontextualization, and redirection of policy into everyday practice—might be caught in the act (Goodson & Lindblad, 2011). Locating inquiry in classrooms is not synonymous with abandoning a contextualized approach or ignoring macro-political and structural power regimes. On the contrary, it is precisely because locating oneself on/in the middle ground is a way to understand these regimes, particularly at times when public intellectuals have been "sent from the room" in terms of their input into policy:

> My way of working is through a very detailed, hard working analysis of the micro and mezzo activities in the world, to develop some theories about what is actually going on. (Goodson, 2011, p. 12)

Ivor recognizes that a response to power may consist in being strategic, by being located in the mezzo layer, and going as far as possible through it to the macro. He is also honest about the fact that:

> the old idea of speaking truth with power that's one way, but another way is a much more manipulative and rather slippery kind of strategic politics. I believe that's what the moment demands. (2011, p. 33)

The Relationship Between Theory and Practice

One of the main sites for investigating the relationship between theory and practice is Ivor's paper "The Educational Researcher as a Public Intellectual" (Goodson, 1999). The contours of the relationship are traced via the history of CARE and the career of its founder, Lawrence Stenhouse. Stenhouse was critical of the location of teacher education in institutions of higher education and of its foundation in its separate constituent disciplines (notably history, philosophy, and psychology). He saw the knowledge generated as divorced from its practical relevance in schools and therefore advocated a model of "applied research" whose aim was not to "dismantle theory altogether but to replace foundational theory with a more engaged theory/practice equation" (Goodson, 1999, p. 286). Ivor in great part agrees with this view. He presents the move of schools of education into faculties of higher education as a "devils bargain" in which real world relevance was traded for the laudable aim of getting teacher education to be seen as a serious matter and the less laudable desire for academic status. However, reinstating theory with the primary aim of making it more relevant to classroom practice went too far in Ivor's view. In the process it overlooked the fact that the relationship between theory and practice is not immutable, but cyclical and tractable. This overreach and oversight had several consequences.

The first of these was that the contribution that foundational disciplinary theory made to practice and its potential to provide answers to "questions of the social position of schooling, the ideological content, the grammar, the social epistemology, the social and political place and purpose of schooling" was lost (Goodson, 1999, p. 287). Following on from this "(b)y focusing back to practice, especially to classroom practices, the doors were open to a new, more utilitarian doctrine" (1999, p. 286).

> Teaching and schooling now could be presented as practical matters beyond broad intellectual contestation. And if teaching is a practical matter, then changing schooling is a matter of technical fine tuning and education research is only there to service the technical adjustments that will deliver effective schools. (p. 287)

What is more, it facilitated an "ideological coup" that had repercussions not just for teacher education and educational research but also for the kind of education that would in the future be on offer:

> By 1980 the forces that had long contested empowering education for all were in control and their desire to extinguish educational theory which engaged questions of the nature and purposes of schooling was evident. For them all arguments for applied and practical research aided in obscuring the larger question of social purpose and social allocation. Progressive arguments were hijacked, inverted and used for a wholly indifferent social project with diametrically opposed purposes. (p. 287)

Although Ivor says that this outcome could not have been anticipated, its effects have nevertheless been all too devastating in terms of inclusive education.

In 1997 when he was considering these issues in preparation for his Lawrence Stenhouse Lecture at the BERA (British Educational Research Association) conference, Ivor was optimistic that the overemphasis on practice would correct itself through new forms of collaboration. As I outlined in the previous chapter powerful global forces and local market forces have served to make him more anxious of late. However, he also takes heart that the implementation of initiatives are subject to the kind of mediation that takes places on the mezzo level of power and that reforms will be refracted through the actions of practitioners who in turn are motivated by their own life politics (Goodson & Anstead, 2010). As we shall see in the next chapter, teachers' concerns over the status of their subject played a significant role in the adoption not only of a subject-based curriculum but also in the form those subjects would take.

This is one reason Ivor has advocated the study of teachers' lives and modes of research that include "the teacher as researcher" and the teacher as "extended professional" (Goodson, 1991a, p. 37). However, this should not be mistaken for "including teachers' voices." He does not privilege teachers nor suggest theirs is the "voice of authority." We are talking instead about giving due regard to teachers without losing sight of the fact that their stories will be influenced by the context in which they are located and by the scripted resources to which they have access. In short, he argues consistently for a collaboration, a dialogue, between theory and practice, which is delivered often by way of a fair trade between researchers and practitioners.

The Personal and the Political

Ivor is consistent in his ideas that, to understand the political, it is imperative to understand an actor's personal life politics and life missions. He has explored these ideas in a number of ways, most trenchantly through his study of educational change and reform, and concluded that policies are often pursued:

> *in spite* of the teacher's personal beliefs and missions. All too often, the "personality of change" has been seen as the "stumbling block" of real reform, rather than as a crucial "building block." (Goodson, 2005a, p. 241, emphasis original)

This can have potentially "catastrophic" consequences. In support of this thesis Ivor cites a meeting with a former teacher of his who had persuaded him many years previously to return to school (1991a). This teacher had proved himself committed to the education of working-class children and therefore Ivor was puzzled by his seeming opposition to curriculum reform that would broaden its appeal to this constituency. Over a pint in the pub, Ivor learnt that this teacher, nearing the end of his career, was no longer willing to place his "centre of gravity" in school. This made sense to me. I felt much the same had happened to me as a teacher when I had my children, which was one facet of a matrix of reasons underpinning my decision to "leave teaching."

Ivor has therefore been at pains to reconceptualize educational research to ensure that "the teacher's voice is heard, heard loudly, heard articulately" (Goodson, 1991a, p. 36). But the challenge is to how to effect it. On this point he is critical of genres of research that focus solely on teachers' representation of themselves, echoing his concerns about an overemphasis on practice devoid of theory. The desire to include teachers' voices has nevertheless led to a "narrative turn" that Ivor sees on the one hand as a welcome antidote to using teachers largely to serve the purposes of researchers' careers and research agendas and that colonizes experiences. Nevertheless he is also wary of representational forms that aim to "empower" but that may be doing the opposite because they are not grounded in an appreciation of the power dynamics of the personal and the political. Ivor summarizes his concerns as follows:

> In educational bureaucracies, power continues to be hierarchically administered. I have often asked administrators and educational bureaucrats why they support personal and practical forms of knowledge for teachers in the form of narratives and stories. Their comments often echo those of the "true believers" in narrative method. But I always go on, after suitable pause and diversion to ask: "What do you do on your leadership courses?" There, it is always "politics as usual" management skills, quality assurance, micro-political strategies, personnel training. *Personal and practical stories for some, cognitive maps of power for others.* So while the use of stories and narratives can provide a useful breathing space away from power, it does not suspend the continuing administration of power; indeed, it could well make this so much easier. Especially as, over time, teachers' knowledge would become more and more personal and practical— different "mentalities," wholly different understandings of power would emerge, as between, say, teachers and school managers, teachers and administrators, teachers and some educational scholars. (1997b, p. 116, emphasis added)

Here we can detect the reason Ivor has been such a staunch advocate of the life history method and it is to this that we now turn.

The Relationship Between Story and Context

Ivor's interest in the life history method is where his ideas about power, theory and practice, the personal and the political, and his insistence on the inclusion of historical knowledge all intersect in a complex matrix of interlocking ideas. Owing much to Mills (1959), Ivor has from the start of his educational research career advocated that understanding the personal and biographical is vital if we are also to understand the social and political. Thus he has researched educational policy and reform, curriculum and schooling, and professionalism through the medium of a study of teachers' lives. His "Life Histories and the Study of Schooling" (1980–1981) did a great deal to foster use of the method in educational settings. However, the need to account for the dynamics of power and to avoid historical amnesia means that this does not entail uncritical acceptance of teachers' unmediated stories. To put it simply, "(s)tories then should not only be narrated but also located" and this involves a "move beyond the self-referential individual narration to a wider contextualized, collaborative mode" (1997b, p. 113).

It is worth reiterating here that this is not just a methodological matter. It might also have real consequences because advocating "stories for some and business as usual for others" risks consolidating power differentials. Moves to include "peripheral voices" may serve only to strengthen power at the center. However, perhaps the greatest danger of ignoring the way in which stories are situated in prevailing social and historical conditions is that it fails to recognize the possibilities for and constraints on our narration that these conditions invoke. At any one time a good part of our narration is through prior scripts and storylines. The (script for the) "coming out story" for example was once not tell-able, and this is even within my living memory. Thus stories can serve to perpetuate, rather than offer the possibility of challenging, those conditions.

Over the next four chapters we will be reading Ivor Goodson through the lens that has been developed so far, locating him in his written works, which will be grouped largely but not slavishly in chronological order. This allows the development of his interests to come to the fore, although it is not positioned as a "progression narrative." It is instead a story of the actions of one public intellectual holding on to what means most to him in the particular and shifting social, historical, and political contexts of his times.

Chapter 5

Life Politics

In short, externally imposed and directed change that fails to take sufficiently into account the "missions" of internal change agents and the increasing force of personal identity projects is likely to founder.

(Goodson et al., 2002, p. 1)

The purpose of this chapter is not exactly aligned to that of the chapters that follow, because the concept of life politics does not enable us to delineate a specific field of research and scholarship in the same way that Ivor's work on curriculum or teachers' lives or narrative does. Life politics is more in the way of an overarching idea, one that has been implicated in the substantive foci to which I will shortly turn and in the methodological genres that Ivor has employed. It is a shorthand, articulating the underlying precepts that, in Ivor's view, should drive the kind of theory building that has relevance in the material world and it provides a vantage point from which the processes of exchange between the micro and the macro might be scrutinized. The reason I have interspersed my account of reading Ivor Goodson with stories about my own experiences and with stories Ivor has told about himself in his writings is precisely to instantiate this point, rather than to provide local color or details that might interest readers or to provide a spot of light relief from engagement with concepts and arguments (although I do think they are also useful in this respect).

Therefore, it sits on top of a chronological approach to "Reading Ivor Goodson" in that it embodies and articulates the enduring features of his scholarship. But presenting it as a corpus of knowledge in its own right, albeit one that has no specific location, rather than as a constituent of the interpretive lens developed earlier, has a number of advantages nonetheless. First and foremost, because the term *life politics* serves as a repository for the constants in Ivor's scholarship, proceeding from here will enable me to lay foundations for subsequent chapters. Second, it helps substantiate the claim that Ivor's entire career must be read as his sustained engagement with issues that have preoccupied him since he was a child, regardless of the angle from which he has approached them or the vantage point from which he has viewed them. In other words, thinking in terms of life politics illuminates the fact that, whatever Ivor has studied, it reflects at heart his preoccupation with the dynamics of the relationship between individuals and the changing sociopolitical contexts in which they are situated. Third, the concept of life politics itself symbolizes those enduring concerns that cut across the various substantive foci of Ivor's work and highlights the way in which there has been consistency, persistence, and coherence in his purpose across multiple sites of engagement. Last but not least, therefore, it offers an entry point to Ivor's own life politics.

There are two key texts that have guided the orientation of this chapter. In *Learning, Curriculum, Life Politics: The Selected Works of Ivor F. Goodson* (2005a), Ivor again brings to the fore his commitment to look back into history to guide and steady his reading of the world, and simultaneously to look forward in anticipation of those aspects of social life that will in the future require greater attention. The title makes explicit that changes in the foci of his scholarship are not to be equated with changes in the thrust of his concerns. Curriculum and life politics stand side by side here. When Ivor's scholarship rotates on its axis, it is a sure sign that he has detected developments on the broader social, cultural, and political landscape that will require attention and action and a relocation to a different site of contestation. He is clear that a failure to act will result in the repositioning and the appropriation of the meaning of one's work by macro-political forces. He therefore sees the requirement to anticipate and be responsive to what is happening in the world as axiomatic in his role as a public intellectual. Indeed he has been impressively prescient. We see, for example, that his analysis that a cultural redefinition, marked by the "reduction of contextual and theoretical discourses and an overall sponsorship of personal and practical forms of discourse and cultural production," was linked to (global) economic restructuring (2005a, p. 188). These ideas are explored in the chapter entitled "The Story So Far" (Goodson, 2005a, pp. 185–199). "The Story So Far" was originally published in the *International Journal of Qualitative Studies in Education* in 1995, and this was in turn a reworking of an earlier unpublished paper. These dates coincide with his relocation from the field of curriculum studies to a more concerted engagement with teachers' lives and professional knowledge. In other words, this relocation signals his awareness that curriculum work was in the process of being repositioned by what was happening on the broader, global stage.

The form and content of the second work that served to guide my reading of Ivor Goodson here is obvious from its title: *Life Politics: Conversations About Education and Culture* (2011). Although it does not make the explicit connections with Ivor's work on curriculum that *Learning, Curriculum, Life Politics* does, the same concern for responsiveness to changes on the global stage is the undertow of each of the conversations included in the volume. The conversational form used to present his ideas models Ivor's concept of the "pedagogic exchange" and positions dialogue as a site for learning. Even in the final chapter, which departs from the "interview" format and is presented in the form of a lecture that Ivor gave in Japan in 2010, the pedagogic exchange is reintroduced by way of a question and answer session that comes at the end of the lecture. In short, this work offers an accessible vehicle for the central tenets of Ivor's life politics and in terms of its substance it foregrounds his ideas about what is happening on the global macro-political stage and in meta-cultural terms.

Some of the pivotal ideas presented in the volume previously mentioned, and particularly his analysis of the rise of rapacious global elites and the intensity of the drive to ever greater consumption, manifested for example in the stratification of education and the atomization of social life, are not those to which Ivor has come recently. Indeed they underpin his long-held belief in the imperative for travel that is inherent in his public intellectual role. Travel is on Ivor's terms unavoidable if he is to respond effectively to phenomena that are simultaneously global in their reach and yet capable of penetrating some of the most private, personal, even intimate areas of life (Berlant, 1997).

Why Life Politics?

In the chapter "Preparing for Postmodernity" (in Goodson, 2005a), Ivor states that life politics equates to "the politics of identity construction and ongoing identity maintenance" (p. 181). This indicates that we are traversing some rough and slippery terrain because identity is, particularly in conditions of postmodernity, a complex, problematic, and contested concept. Sometimes it is interpreted in ways that are, or have the potential to be, at odds with Ivor's scholarly intentions and/or with his life politics, and therefore there is the danger that he could be misread. But it is important to appreciate that the notion of life politics was a feature even of his early work on curriculum and was articulated in his inclusion of teachers in his analyses of curriculum formation and in his parallel focus on teachers' lives and careers (Goodson & Ball, 1989). When he began to focus more intensively on teachers' lives it did not signal a change in his concerns or the reconfiguration of his enduring preoccupations. It simply manifested his recognition that the antecedent and underlying factors that undermine social justice could now be better observed, and pursued in a more meaningful way, on a different site.

This meant that, from the start of the 1990s, Ivor's attention began to turn from the study of curriculum as a way of accessing the social role of schooling and to focus more on "life politics" and how this played out in relation to social, historical, and geographical contexts. There was in short a recalibration of his hopes for the role of education. It meant that he no longer saw the study of curriculum as a significant way to the achievement of a more just society. Understanding why this happened *when it did* is fundamental to any meaningful reading of his work. It must be read as a story of action within the context of changes in the sociopolitical circumstances at the time and the related postmodern turn.

The Turn to Life Politics: A Response to Changes in the Sociopolitical Context

Crucial to understanding the significance of Ivor's shifting his attention from curriculum to teachers' lives, and from there to narrative, is the sense that we are apprehending him at a particular historical moment in a specific location, which also involves going further back in time to the UK in the mid-1970s and to what was a watershed moment in its sociopolitical history. The economic position resembled that in which several European countries find themselves today. The UK government, faced with the prospect of the country becoming bankrupt, applied to the International Monetary Fund (IMF) for loans. These were granted, but with conditions attached that would impact not only on economic but also on social policy, insofar as control of inflation and expenditure would now take center stage with a shift away from the goal of full employment and social welfare. This is not the place to consider whether this reading of the economic situation was or is "the truth," or whether it was right or wrong to accept these conditions. The point is that it led to a sea change in the direction of political will and to the start of a longer period of change in the political climate and social structures in the UK.

Ivor makes a compelling case that changes on the macro level have an impact on mezzo and micro levels. "Mezzo" in this sense comprises institutions such as schools, the church, family, and so on, and "micro" encompasses the individual and personal level, and it is precisely these that have been dismantled as the "mediating membrane" between global forces and the individual. I will return to expand and consider the implications of this point in the next two chapters, but we have already touched on how such changes are manifested in one way in the process of repositioning. By the 1990s, in the specific circumstances of the UK, therefore, curriculum scholarship was no longer imbued with the same potential to contribute to or impact on agendas for social justice. In other words, it was no longer a site on which the war for inclusion and social justice would be fought, which is not to say it will not be resurrected in the future. Indeed Ivor has recently *re*turned to a focus on curriculum in the context of his work on narrative (Goodson, in press). But, in the changed sociopolitical circumstances of the time, it would have been pointless for curriculum scholars simply to carry on regardless.

As a social and economic historian, therefore, but also as a self-confessed shrewd operator, Ivor was aware that discussions were being conducted and decisions made in rooms to which curriculum scholars no longer had access, behind doors that were locked to them (Goodson, 2011, p. 38). He recognized that if his endeavors as a public intellectual were to have continued relevance he would similarly have to refocus his efforts. It is important to reiterate that concerns about the relevance of his work are firmly attached to his own understanding of his role as a public intellectual because they foreground the moral aspects of his desire for relevance. On these terms it is always and already a commitment to social and political ends rather than the pursuit of career advancement and financial gain, as pleasant as these rewards undoubtedly are.

It cannot be overstated that the moral and intellectual aspects of Ivor's work as a public intellectual are indistinguishable. The postmodern textual practice of conjoining words with a slash is useful here so that when we say *public intellectual* we are always and already invoking its intellectual/moral aspects. Ivor is upfront in stating that he enjoys the earthly rewards of a distinguished career. But if this had been his main motivation, first, he could have chosen a less contentious or challenging field in which to make his mark (and he did in fact abandon a career as an academic historian because it did not speak to his sense of mission). Second, he could have retired long before now, instead of pursuing a punishing schedule as a traveling, organic intellectual.

Ivor's response to sea-changes on the macro-political scene can therefore be interpreted as representing a story of action within this changing context, a manifestation of how his theoretical perspective on the workings of power were translated into a lived response to its transformations on a broader stage. I am using the word *response* rather than *reaction* here because, to reiterate, Ivor's independence is a major feature of his modus operandi. He follows his own scholarly agenda even while remaining aware of the way in which this will be positioned in the wider world. His adherence to life history when government ministers were demanding quantitative research is testament to that alone.

Holding on to his own position, even while acknowledging the contribution of other schools of thought and the theoretical perspectives of other scholars, is likewise a defining feature of Ivor's scholarship. Ivor is a generous reader, engaging respectfully with other theoretical positions and displaying what Andrew Sparkes (2009) refers to as "connoisseurship." This goes against the grain of much academic practice, where it is usual to mark out one's position by highlighting its differences with, even superiority to, other positions. He references, for example, the contribution made by feminist thought in general, by feminist historians in particular, and by Carolyn Steedman (1986) specifically, to the development of linkages between stories and their contexts. However, he still adheres to his own methods of exploring them. This feature of his modus operandi, his adoption of a "both and" position, is also apparent in his response to what is often referred to as the postmodern turn.

Life Politics in the Context of Postmodernism

In addition to the changing social, economic, and political environment of the 1970s, 1980s, and 1990s, there is another aspect to the historical moment in which the reorientation of Ivor's scholarship must be located. Concomitant with sociopolitical and economic changes, and in Ivor's view intimately related to them, was the turn to the postmodern, and he is explicit in framing the significance of life politics as a response to, or more specifically preparation for, postmodernity (Goodson, 2005a, pp. 181–186). It is typical that Ivor recognized how the postmodern posed "perils" *and* offered "promises" for the world of education (2005a, p. 181). He therefore acknowledged that this would entail a reconfiguration of the field of battle, stating that:

> some of the median associations such as universities and schools may well be diminished and decoupled in significant ways so that institutional sites may not be any longer the only significant sites of struggle . . . more important for the future will be the site of *personal life and identity.* (2005a, p. 181, emphasis added)

I have placed emphasis on the above because it is here that the potential for misconstruing Ivor's meaning is great.

I want to make absolutely clear from the start that he is not now advocating a retreat from concerns about the social and it is no coincidence that life *politics* was the term he chose in which to encapsulate these ideas. In the first place he is not stating that institutional sites are no longer relevant only that their relevance is diminished. Neither is he advocating a total re-location of scholarly interest from the institutional to the individual. He states that *both* sites need attention, but that, in the context of postmodernism, focusing on the institutional may be less efficacious than focusing on the individual or, to be more specific, on the relationship between the two. In other words, Ivor's is neither a wholehearted *embrace* of the postmodern nor a rejection of it. In keeping with his modus operandi it is a strategic and pre-active *response* to it.

His preparations for postmodernism therefore did not include abandoning that which was previously important to him, and he still views phenomena and experiences through his social constructionist lens (Goodson et al., 2002; Goodson & Anstead, 2010). We can hardly talk here of his "leaving" or "moving away" particular fields of inquiry. His shift in focus from curriculum onto teachers does not represent a break with the past or a total redirection and reformulation of his scholarly mission. Shifting his gaze from curriculum, to teachers' lives, and, later, to the study of narrative signifies his recognition that if he is to fulfill this mission he must anticipate where the most effective response to changes in the sociopolitical climate might be located.

The idea that turning from curriculum to life politics in its various guises and on different sites of inquiry represents only a shift in focus and not a fundamental change in mission is also supported by the fact that Ivor has not only *declared* himself resistant to progression narratives and to influences that are at odds with his allegiance to his background, but has *shown* himself to be so as well. He did not, for example, buy into the aspirational discourse of "the scholarship boy," the clever son of working-class parents who went to grammar school. It was not simply that he did not buy into the story that grammar school would lead him to a "better" life. More than this, he explicitly rejected what that life represented, which was a repudiation of his origins. It is little wonder then that he left school at 15 with one qualification (in history) to go and work in a crisp factory. Indeed, rather than being framed as a progression narrative his experiences at grammar school served only to raise more questions about the disjunctures between his world and that one. I will pick up Ivor's reflections on these early experiences of resistance to the script of the scholarship boy in the chapter on narrative. What is salient here is the fact that the concerns he brought to this area of his scholarly work had such long roots.

Likewise, the story he relates about his daily journey to school in the morning and back home at the end of the day is one of an actual and metaphorical border crossing into a different, middle-class milieu and marks the (conscious) start of his interest in the idea of displacement (Goodson, 2011). Standing out in his own community by virtue of his school uniform, he took to stuffing his blazer and yellow-tassled school cap into his saddle bag for the bike ride to school, donning them only when he got there (2005a, p. 17). He also tells that he stood out as different in grammar school thanks to his accent and use of dialect, his cultural referents, his worldviews, and his politics. His scholarly interrogation of life politics has its roots in the fact that he had to think early in his life about who he was (2011, p. 43) because he was not like most other boys at his school.

The Study of Life Politics as a Transcendent Practice

The above account makes more explicit some of the conflicting ideas that the juxtaposition of "life" with "politics" presages. Having their origins in the concerns of his childhood, articulated as a sense of mission and realized in his work as a public intellectual, they compel him to take a stance that emphasizes the importance of the collective over the individual. On the other hand, using personal experiences, particularly those concerned with identity formation, privileges the individual and idiosyncratic, even if and when their intended function is as an entry point to an engagement with broader social issues. How is it possible then for Ivor to utter the words *life* and *politics* in the same breath? The answer owes a great deal to his use of life history and to the fact that his theorizing is firmly rooted in what he calls the middle ground, the point of exchange where, to reference Mills, public issues become personal troubles. Ivor's scholarship, which entails bringing the individual and the social, the personal and the political, and the structural and experiential into close proximity, is also a means of slackening the tension between them. It offers a way to reconcile conflicting lines of argument, which in turn opens up spaces for fresh perspectives, furnishes the opportunity for deeper insights, and extends theoretical reach. Proceeding now from this basic understanding of his position I will outline some of the key points with respect to the concept of identity housed within the overarching concept of life politics.

Life Politics in the Contested Terrain of Identity

In the chapter "Preparing for Postmodernity," then, Ivor set out the significance of identity as "a major and growing site of ideological and intellectual contestation" in the context of globalization and the conditions of postmodernity. Whereas identity once conveyed a sense of attachment to particular roles or status positions, in the conditions of postmodernity identity becomes emergent, an "ongoing narrative project," articulated in Giddens's (1991) notion of the reflexive project of the self. Ivor's response to this transformation has been strategic, declaring that it involves both dangers and opportunities, or *perils* and *promises* to use his terms, for the world of education. However, this should not be misconstrued as a wholehearted engagement with identity politics or an uncritical acquiescence in its ramifications for broader structural concerns.

I have already set out some of the ways in which Ivor is able to maintain his commitment to his life's mission with/in the upheavals wrought by changes in socioeconomic policy and postmodern thought and how he is able to exploit its promises while exposing and sidestepping its perils. In particular, his use of life history, which requires not only the narration of life stories but more specifically the deployment of the devices of location and collaboration, furnishes the opportunity to maintain the dynamic of the structural and the agentic. In other words, attending to the social history and social geography of experience and to *stories* of experience and the circumstances in which they originate and are narrated, allows him to simultaneously exploit the advantages of the postmodern focus on the self while avoiding a retreat into interiority.

I want to animate this assertion now with specific reference to ideas of identity, inasmuch as identity can be construed as a representation or manifestation of the self. We have already noted that Ivor does not think of himself as a multiple self (Moriarty, 2012). Indeed it would be curious if he were to profess to working in a modality of holding if he did not have this sense of enduring selfhood. However, this statement does not stand in contradistinction to the ideas of the emergent and multiple self of postmodernism because the constancy to which Ivor refers is not a feature of selfhood as an entity. It is instead a feature of identity as a narrative. Ivor states unequivocally that he sees "identity as keeping *a* meaningful narrative going" (2011, p. 48). This conceptualization sits at the heart of his understanding of life politics, because it contains the possibility that responsiveness to change and loyalty to a set of core values and beliefs are not mutually exclusive. It is this sense of selfhood that we see him enacting in his own life and in the consistency of concern he brings to different sites of engagement. But beyond this, the importance of conceptualizing selfhood as enduring narrative resides in the fact it can be used in a transcendent way in interrogating the operation of power in social life.

There are numerous examples of the way in which Ivor has used the notion of consistency in his own selfhood in this transcendent way. His bike ride to school that I referred to earlier has been used as an entry point into understanding the processes and experiences of "border crossings," for instance. However, the example that stands out for me is contained in an almost throwaway remark he made to Moriarty (2012). He tells her that when he went to the prestigious London School of Economics as a student he turned up wearing Teddy Boy garb, a style of clothing associated with working-class boys at the end of the 1950s and beginning of the 1960s. Perhaps it is because my older brother was similarly attired in those days, and even now is wont to don his blue suede shoes, but this was to my mind a powerful evocation of the concept of holding on and a manifestation of the consistency in Ivor's selfhood. We can detect in this act his refusal to participate in the aspirational discourse of higher education and we are made aware that being dressed as a Teddy Boy somehow set him apart from most of his contemporaries (it is hard to imagine the middle-class Mick Jagger, who also attended the LSE at the time, ever being similarly attired).

All this is important, but this seemingly small detail is endowed with still greater potency and explanatory power because from here we are able to go on to ask questions about why it should be that such modes of dress were out of place in this institution. This in turn creates a vantage point for observing the processes of exchange between lived reality and socio-structural factors and individual negotiations (or mediations) within them. I would also venture to say that proceeding from seemingly trivial and mundane details of everyday life to enable interrogation of social processes sets Ivor apart from those, particularly cultural, theorists who are exploring similar ideas about identity in the context of critiques of postmodernity. To substantiate this point I will briefly test Ivor's contention that he is not a multiple self against Celia Lury's (1998) notion of "prosthetic culture," an idea taken forward by Bev Skeggs (2004) in her exploration of selfhood.

The prosthetic self, as the term suggests, stands in contrast to the concept of a self comprised of core values, desires, beliefs, and morals. It is instead a detachable self and is achieved by "trying on" identities through the appropriation of particular resources, often, but not exclusively, cultural. This form of selfhood is not available to all. Only some have sufficient access to these resources and here Skeggs (2004) implicates the structural factors of class, race, gender, ethnicity, and antecedent power dynamics. She uses an example from the film *Pulp Fiction* to animate her argument, arguing that John Travolta is able to appropriate a racialized notion of "cool" for the duration of the film but can divest himself of it after that. Samuel L. Jackson, however, is always and already defined as "cool" and his access to other identities proscribed.

This is a powerful illustration of Skeggs's (2004) argument, but to my mind Ivor's transcendent use of detail from everyday life, such as being dressed as a Teddy Boy when he went to his prestigious university, is a more economical, more accessible, and more powerful way of highlighting and interrogating the same issues and of connecting issues of identity with lived realities. In short, Ivor's recognition of the importance of identity simultaneously acknowledges the importance of working with/in the conditions of postmodernity and reconfigures the terms of engagement in doing so. Identity is not significant per se. It is significant in its provision of a portal by which to access the underlying and overarching power dynamics *and* the underlying and overarching processes that engender them. This is the function that including life politics in analyses of social life serves and why it has been a consistent feature of Ivor's approach no matter where he has situated his social inquiries. It is with this in mind therefore that we will now proceed to a reading of the substantive areas of Ivor's scholarship, starting with curriculum before moving to his study of teachers' lives and professional knowledge and finally to his exploration of narrative.

Chapter 6

Curriculum

You have to decide early in life whose side you're on. And given my own history, it has always remained obvious to me that I would remain on the side of the group I came from.

(Goodson, 2011, p. 3)

There have been few, if any, aspects of curriculum that Ivor has not interrogated, unpacked, reenergized, and reconceptualized: curriculum history (Goodson, 1984, 1985, 1990a); curriculum policy and reform (1989, 1990b); the history and significance of school subjects and subject knowledge (1981, 1983, 1987, 1991b, 1992a, 1992b; Goodson, Anstead & Mangan, 1998); methodological issues (1980–1981, 1990c, 2009a); international perspectives on curriculum (1988); and even its etymology (1995, 1997c). Although Ivor's preoccupation with curriculum predates it, the publication of *School Subjects and Curriculum Change* in 1983 (based on his doctoral research) can be said to mark the beginning of Ivor's scholarly involvement with it. In this book he posited school subjects not as monolithic entities enshrining Knowledge, but as social constructions that reflected, and were the means of achieving, the aspirations of external structuring forces and the institutional responses to those. But this work, which is even now still in publication, was not just significant in its own right. Its impact extends far beyond its own singular contribution, serving as the catalyst and impetus for other works that aimed to study curriculum as a site of social contestation and distribution from a socio-historical perspective (www.ivorgoodson.com). Particularly significant here is a series of more than 20 works that are gathered under the banner of Studies in Curriculum History, which was commissioned by Falmer Press in 1984 and of which Ivor was series editor. Ivor told me he is particularly proud of this series, as the collected works consolidated a way of studying and thinking about curriculum that began with *School Subjects*.

Ivor contributed four books to the series. *Defining the Curriculum* (Goodson & Ball, 1984) explored what happens at the various levels of curriculum formation (national, institutional, classroom, and personal) in the making of school subjects. *The Making of Curriculum* (1995), which was being put together more than a decade earlier than this date of publication, during the planning of the National Curriculum in England, provides a response to theories that concentrate either on implementation or on resistance at the micro level. It was an attempt to "go back to go" (p. xv), to trace the historical antecedents of the "new" national curriculum and to include the motives and aspirations of the reformers in analyses, and also those of teachers, something which had been largely absent from other analyses. In this book Ivor also highlights the way curriculum history enhances understanding of schooling and the way in which it works in mutually complementary ways with histories of pedagogy. *Studying School Subjects* (Goodson & Marsh, 1996) provided a guidebook and introduction to the work that had been going on in the field of the study of school subjects, providing socio-historical perspectives on them and on subject traditions and subject departments. *Subject Knowledge* (Goodson, Anstead, & Mangan, 1998) brought much-needed international perspectives to the study of school subjects and reflected Ivor's recognition of the increasing insinuation of global stratifying forces exercised at the micro level.

The selection of works that I have referenced and those that I have summarized here, along with *School Subjects and Curriculum Change,* which I will turn to in more detail presently, is not intended to be exhaustive or comprehensive or to suggest it captures the reach and depth of Ivor's ideas. But it does form the bedrock of his research and thinking on curriculum and highlights the difficulties entailed in trying to capture or catalogue his long involvement across the vast terrain of curriculum scholarship. Rather than attempting to provide a broad and general overview I will concentrate on what was and is distinctive about his study of all the various aspects of curriculum. Although any approach to representing such a huge contribution to the field will necessarily involve omissions, I would argue that directing our attention here will at least provide some of the essence of his scholarship.

There are two things to bear in mind before proceeding to a consideration of what gives Ivor's curriculum scholarship its essential flavor, or its Ivor-ness as I came to think of it. First, Ivor did not set out to make a name for himself as a curriculum scholar. In conversations I have had with him he seems genuinely surprised that *School Subjects and Curriculum Change* had the impact it did. He was to his mind simply documenting what he considered to be commonsense knowledge about how curriculum comes to be made and implemented. Second, although I focus on what I consider to be the distinctive features of his work, I am not suggesting they are all unique to his approach. For example, Ivor was not alone in conceptualizing curriculum as a social construction that served the perpetuation of hegemonic circuits of power rather than as an educational construction whose primary purpose is to engage learners. However, I would argue that, taken together, certain aspects of his curriculum scholarship serve to give it a unique character and personality and that this should in turn be read in the context of the times in which it was located.

Auto/biography and Personal Life Politics

For Ivor the study of curriculum was intensely personal. He brought to it his experiences not only as a teacher but also as a member of a tribe who had the certain knowledge that schools and schooling were not there to foster their interests or well-being. Therefore the origins of Ivor's interrogation of curriculum can in one sense be traced back to his early days at primary school. I was moved to tears by his depiction of children clinging screaming to their mothers' bicycles and to gate posts at the prospect of entering through the school gates (Goodson, 2005a), probably because I had a little cry in the toilets at school almost every day until I was more than 12 years old, if I wasn't able to convince my mother to let me stay at home. Such was my sense of being in a hostile place.

I also found it moving to read about the questions he thought school would be there to answer because, unsophisticated as he says they are, they get at the heart of the human cost of class-inflected power relations:

> Why did my father work so hard? Why did I not see him in the mornings, or until late in the evening? Why did my mother go to work to "support me"? Why were all the fields I played in being developed by more and larger "council estates"? Why did we have to walk (or later, ride) more than three miles to school? Why was the school in a "posh" village and not in my village? Why were the children from my village treated differently to the children from the immediate school locality? (2005a, p. 17)

Although his questions became more sophisticated as he grew older, in essence they still asked why school-based learning was so far removed from issues that would not only engage the hearts and minds of learners (Goodson & Deakin Crick, 2009) but also educate for an effective challenge to these iniquities and for the creation of a fairer society.

The beginnings of his own "vision and version of schooling in general and curriculum in particular" (Goodson, 2009b, p. 91) were therefore forged in these early experiences and they suffuse his preoccupation with curriculum. Hence his belief that it was a key site on which the battle for social justice was being fought and could still be won predated and transcended the influence of tutors such as Basil Bernstein and Michael Young at the Institute of Education. It was imbibed instead during his formative years, as the child of working-class parents and in the particular experiences of his childhood, including those at school and on the production line. It is the articulation and manifestation of his life politics, the outcome of his holding on to the values and beliefs that were forged there, the response to his everyday experience of practices, particularly schooling, that far from serving to include his people, served instead to exclude and even oppress them. It is what the people of his tribe just know. Ivor states that what he does may be taken for scholarship in the academy but for the people of his tribe this would just be "common sense."

This early mediating experience was augmented by his experiences of teaching in, by all accounts, radical comprehensive schools, first Countesthorpe in Leicestershire and then as head of humanities at Stantonbury Campus in Milton Keynes. His decision to become a teacher, instead of continuing a fledgling career as an academic historian, must itself have been momentous for someone who had known, as Ivor had, the grinding monotony of the production line. Many, if not most, teachers today would find it inexplicable that he saw teaching as a way to reconcile the dichotomy between "life" and "study" that he had felt as a history lecturer (2009b, p. 93). But his decision not only points to the strength of his enduring commitment to his "mission" to act for the people of his tribe, it also says much about the prevailing political and social climate at the time. In short, Ivor had entered the Institute of Education in London when there was, if not commitment, then at least sufficient goodwill toward inclusive education.

The collision between the ideals of his mission and the lived reality of schools that he saw as suffering from "contextual inertia" ultimately led Ivor back to the academy. That schools could remain so inured or resistant to change when, on a broader social and political canvas, the move was in the direction of change required an explanation, one that was rooted in the everyday lived realities of teachers in schools and that spoke to commonsense understandings. On one level then his relocation into the academy was a strategic move, a redirection of his energies from school-based action to academic research. However, he was still working toward the goal of social justice and in this sense his strategy was driven by his prefigurative politics. Prefigurative politics, a term Ivor borrows from Breines (1980), "seeks to create and sustain within the lived practice of the movement relationships and political forms that 'prefigure' and embody the desired society" (p. 421). In other words, and I am continuing the argument I set out in the previous chapter, combining the strategic with the prefigurative has been a defining characteristic of his entire scholarly career and not just of his curriculum scholarship. His underlying motivation and his consistent and enduring preoccupation has always been with social justice and the achievement of an inclusive society, regardless of where it may have led him.

Ivor's longevity alone is testament to his success at marrying the prefigurative with the strategic but it is important to point out the difference here between Breines's notions of prefigurative and strategic politics and the idea that "the end justifies the means," because the latter is largely devoid of the moral element that is the heart of the former. Prefigurative politics requires not only embedding core values in the ends toward which one is working but also "holding on" to those values throughout the process of their realization. In this respect, Ivor did not so much embrace Breines's concept as use it to articulate that which already sat at the heart of his way of being in the world.

The Restoration of History to Theory

When Ivor entered the field of curriculum studies in the latter half of the 1970s he found it modulated by the scholarship of the previous decade. Sociologists of the 1960s had laid some conceptual foundations for treating curriculum as a social construction, but they had done so during a period of instability, when the whole Western world was in a state of flux, and when the possibilities for change, for revolution even, seemed within reach (Goodson, 1989). Ivor saw this as problematic, although he was fully committed to the need to make curricula more inclusive. He was also concerned that the impetus toward transformation, reform, or revolution had been accompanied by the evacuation of the theoretical "high ground" where those aspects of curriculum that were stable and seemed unchallengeable were located, and by a concomitant relocation to the "low ground" of the classroom as the "centre of action" and the "arena of resistance" (1989, p. 133).

He was particularly concerned that abandoning the high ground had resulted in the loss of historical perspectives, and specifically the knowledge that curriculum development had been a story of continuities rather than of ruptures with the past. There was, for example, a startling convergence of both substance and rhetoric between the National Curriculum in England in the 1980s and the Secondary Regulations that appeared in 1904 on the back of the 1902 Education Act. At the same time he was also critical of philosophy's reluctance to come down from the high ground and its failure to admit the salience of what was going on in schools and classrooms. Philosophy had also failed to pay sufficient regard to historical perspectives. To Ivor's mind, the most fruitful place to stand was on the "middle ground," the meeting place of both the enduring features and everyday practice of curriculum.

He therefore insisted in restoring a (socio)historical perspective to the study of curriculum. This amounts to far more than simply "raiding history" (Goodson, 1984, p. 26). Instead it is a way of calling attention to the ways in which historical amnesia (1989) is both a symptom and a cause of the failure to deal adequately with the moving target of curriculum (re)formation (Goodson & Marsh, 1996). By taking an Annaliste approach to the study of history, Ivor conceptualizes events not as moments *in* time but as representative of cycles and continuities *over* time. The short, medium, and longer term effects of these cycles are akin to the swells and currents that occur at different ocean depths (Goodson, 2005b). By incorporating these Annaliste conceptualizations of time, Ivor was able to restore a focus on the continuities and stabilities in the nature and character of curriculum. For example, he proceeded from an understanding that the challenge to the bipartite system of education at the end of the 1960s and beginning of the 1970s, although capturing popular and political commitment to a more egalitarian society at the time, did not actually represent a break with the past.

Having stated that my aim is not specifically to argue for the uniqueness of Ivor's curriculum scholarship, it is precisely this historical sensibility that Joe Kincheloe (1997) highlights as marking it out. To illustrate his point Kincheloe points out that, like William Pinar and the Reconceptualists in the

US, "Goodson appreciated that the future of the field would revolve around understanding not technical curriculum development" (p. x.). Ivor also followed Pinar's example in pursuing the etymology of the word *curriculum* as a verb (Goodson, 1995) and by making the connections between this understanding of curriculum as a course to be run and pedagogies of transmission that close off avenues to more interactive pedagogies. By setting his analysis in its historical context, however, Kincheloe (1997) maintains that Ivor added a much needed dimension to Pinar's phenomenological approach:

> Synchronic analysis—snapshots of complex processes at a particular moment—cannot compensate for extended analysis over time. Indeed, such snapshots, Goodson contends, may actually mislead curriculum scholars attempting to trace the evolutionary process. Only through a careful historical analysis can explanation be developed. Theoretical explanation should not drive historical scholarship, Ivor admonishes, but the identification of the recurrence of historical events can elucidate theoretical explanation. Goodson's subtle understanding of these historiographical and social theoretical dynamics is instructive for curriculum scholars and (sic) well as students of history and sociology. (p. xvi)

In short, by including a historical dimension Ivor extended his theoretical reach and added analytical depth to the study of curriculum.

The Focus on Subjects, Not Knowledge

Ivor's experience in schools led him to conclude that a focus on individual subjects, rather than on curriculum as a homogeneous whole, provided a point of entry not only to understanding the mechanics but also the dynamics of curriculum formation, particularly the power dynamics involved (Goodson, 1983). He formulated three hypotheses about school subjects that underpinned his subsequent treatments of them. The first of these was that school subjects are not monolithic entities, not "timeless statements of intrinsically worthwhile content" (1987, p. 10) but shifting alliances and amalgamations of subgroups and traditions whose influence serves to change the boundaries and priorities of subject knowledge. The second posited that in the process of establishing a school subject the move is away from utilitarian and pedagogic traditions toward a culminating "academic" discipline, a process conceptualized as "academic drift." The third is that subjects defend their own academic status and simultaneously seek to exclude other contenders from establishing their own claims to eminence.

Against the backdrop of these hypotheses he conceptualized schools themselves as battlegrounds. He highlighted that alliances are formed between academic subjects, academic examinations, and able pupils and between exam boards, subject teachers, and subject associations. He supported with actual examples his contention that the battles for the academic status of subjects and the resources and rewards this attracts was the basis for theorizing curriculum. In other words, his analysis was located not in lofty ideas about the nature of knowledge but in the arena of lived realities. It was a reality of which I have personal recall. As Ivor points out, those battles were not motivated by thoughts of the innate relevance of those subjects and the nature of the knowledge they enshrined, or by their appeal to pupils, but by the pursuit of material and self-interests.

It is important to clarify here how we are to understand the role of teachers in these battles. Ivor has offered a clear rebuttal of any interpretation that positions teachers as primary power players in them or that takes their pursuit of status and resources to imply that they are *generally* self-interested individuals:

> Nothing could be further from the truth. But the bureaucratization and structuration of schooling leaves the groups or associations which represent teachers with little choice but to pursue status and resources. To do otherwise is to condemn colleagues and students to low status and poor resources. (Goodson, 1997a, p. xvi)

In other words, "teachers are often ill-served by those who control schooling" (1997a, p. xvi).

Ivor has therefore drawn attention to the recursive process of establishing the legitimacy of school subjects in creating a vehicle for promoting specific forms of (examinable) knowledge. He has not only interrogated the role of the subject knowledge enshrined therein in the formation of curriculum, but he has done so in such a way that exposes the real work and tactical maneuvering by interested parties. It is they who set curricular parameters so that school subjects enshrine and perpetuate the academic traditions from which they emanate. A key element in this theoretical development was to highlight the battles over subject knowledge that went on *within* as well as *between* subjects. It is here that the theaters of engagement are located in the first instance outside schools before they are relocated in schools to be enacted in departmental meetings and classrooms.

Ivor reaches again to historical precedent, specifically the case of school science, to make this point (Goodson, 1995). Drawing on the work of David

Layton (1973), he highlights that the content of science subjects did not evolve as a response to questions about what would be the most useful or even interesting kind of science to teach to pupils. Were this the case it is likely that school science would have proceeded, for example, from a curriculum based on the "Science of Common Things," which was in turn rooted in the everyday experiences of those being taught and that enjoyed some success when it was offered to mainly working-class pupils in elementary schools in the nineteenth century. In fact, the Science of Common Things was so successful that it raised the possibility of working-class children being better educated in science than their social "superiors." Lord Wrottesley, chair of a Parliamentary Committee of the British Association for the Advancement of Science, articulates the concerns of the ruling class when he states that:

> It would be an unwholesome and vicious state of society in which those who are comparatively unblessed with nature's gifts should be generally superior in intellectual attainments to those above them in station. (quoted in Goodson, 1995, p. 21)

Lest the power of those supposedly superior in station be in doubt, shortly after this pronouncement—made in 1860—science was removed from the elementary curriculum.

School science, when it reappeared, was a "watered down" version of pure laboratory science that in turn became:

> accepted as the *correct* view of science, a view which has persisted, largely unchallenged, to the present day. Science, as a school subject, was powerfully redefined to become similar in form to so much else in the secondary curriculum— pure, abstract, a body of knowledge enshrined in syllabuses and textbooks. (1995, p. 21, original emphasis)

Therefore, far from being the result of a natural evolution, we see that social production and reproduction, social distribution of schooling, social and political priorities, and the control and operation of school and classroom are all implicated in the content of school subjects (1995, p. 21). We see here, in short, the enactment of Ivor's proposition that subject content resonates with the dynamics of a power struggle that was always and already weighted against social justice.

The Inclusion of Teachers

Ivor considered the failure to include teachers and what he came to call their life politics as a significant omission in theories of curriculum formation. They are, after all, responsible for curriculum practices on a daily basis. A failure to include teachers in analyses of curriculum was producing abstract, generalized, and universalized theories that made no sense to teachers in their everyday lives, and not just in their professional lives. But quite apart from that, curriculum scholarship devoid of the presence of teachers was failing to answer some pressing and interlinked questions: If a dominant, subject-based curriculum was not meeting the needs of the vast majority of pupils in schools, in whose interests did it function? If curriculum is a social construction, who was constructing it and why? Why was it proving so resilient and impervious to certain actions on the broader stage, to ideological, political, cultural, and social shifts and transformations? After all, it would be reasonable to suppose that the opposite would be the case, that curriculum would be unable to resist the weight brought to bear by those contextual shifts and transformations.

Ivor's approach to addressing these omissions was to set in conversation the story of his experiences as a teacher in school with theories that made sense of it. To his mind these theories were not located in the realm of the sociology of knowledge or in the primacy of universities to determine what was taught in schools. Equally, he did not privilege the primacy of "insider knowledge," although he relocated inquiry to schools, to the site where the battles over curriculum were taking place. He argued that curriculum was not made through the efforts of universities to control knowledge but in schools, in the battles over resources. He emphasized how these battles played out in the lives of individual teachers. He included, for example, the life history of "Sean Carson," whose struggles to establish environmental studies as a subject that might be examined at A level led to him becoming ill and retiring prematurely (1980–1981). But this was not presented as one man's individualized battle. Sean Carson's story served instead as a conduit to understanding the power relations inherent in the fight for subject legitimacy.

In his role as a public intellectual, Ivor is always mindful of the relevance of his work. Therefore, taking the approach that he did is not simply a scholarly or intellectual matter. He has set out, often, the consequences for educational practice in general and for curriculum formation specifically when teachers feel themselves alienated from theories that "collide" with their lived realities. But equally, a "pendulum swing" away from theory can in turn produce a specific kind of practice, one that can be paraphrased as "doing the job better." I will take up this point more fully in the next chapter but in his work on professional lives, Ivor charted how a sense of vocation and professionalism, even of mission and passion, among teachers who entered the profession between the 1950s and 1980s has been eroded over time. There has been such a change in the ecology of teaching that contemporary cohorts now see it largely as "just a job," its significance divorced from the rest of their lives and from that which really matters to them (Goodson, 2007).

Let us not forget, moreover, that we are talking about other "real lives" here, too. For many children, if not most of them, school continues to be an alienating test of endurance. While "disengaged" is most frequently allied to "disadvantaged" in some prevalent discourses, I listened with a sinking heart as my own 12-year-old son explained with simple honesty why he was also disengaged with school and failing to "realize his potential." "It's just so boring and pointless," was his explanation. And this from a boy whose parents are or were both teachers and who is now a graduate. Sadly, however, I found myself agreeing with his analysis. Had I not felt much the same alienation as a pupil in my first years at school and the same frustration as a teacher?

The need to start from the experience of teachers' lived realities is therefore crucial in revitalizing commitments to social justice. But let us be clear here. Ivor does not say that teachers are party to superior knowledge, that it is sufficient merely to let them speak these "truths," grounded in everyday experience, to come to a fully formed theory of curriculum formation and practice. Indeed this may lead instead to a reinforcement of those discourses that we may wish to challenge. Inclusion of the teacher's voice is not the whole story. Ivor is insistent that what teachers say is described by the parameters in which they are speaking, influenced by the requirement to deal with the exigencies and negotiations of daily life and susceptible to the rehearsal and repetition of "scripts," the dominant and prevailing storylines whose availability often forecloses on potential counternarratives. But paying attention to the parameters in which stories of personal experience are told does not equate to denigrating or dismissing their contribution to understanding. Our starting point is the argument for their inclusion. But it does signal that Ivor's commitment to "bringing the teachers back in" (Goodson, 1997b) is nuanced, multidimensional, and relational to the context in which it is executed.

On the one hand these ideas have led Ivor to methodological conclusions. If, as he argued, teachers were implicated in (but, to reiterate, not responsible for) the perpetuation of particular forms of curriculum, it was imperative to find a way of incorporating these perspectives without simultaneously sidelining the importance of contextualized theories to explain their origins and locations. He therefore reached to life history methods that not only allowed inclusion but also interrogation of teachers' understandings, perceptions, and perspectives. He also advocated a collaborative approach between teachers in schools and researchers in schools of education, which was more than the provision of stories by the former and theories by the latter. The "fair trade" of the different contributions offered by teachers and researchers led, on Ivor's terms, to the expansion and transformation of the parameters to understanding of both. For example, by focusing on teachers' location at the intersection of policy and practice, but not forgetting the influence of their individual life politics, Ivor developed a profound understanding of the "ecology" of public service and how this has changed in response to the "climate change" in public policy (Goodson, 2007).

Attention to Power Dynamics

When the talk is of wars and alliances as it is in Ivor's curriculum scholarship, it is surely a sign that we are talking about issues of power. Understanding power, how it is conceptualized, and how it operates is the undercurrent to each of the ideas outlined earlier. His preoccupation with power sits at the heart of his scholarly endeavors and not only cuts across his curriculum scholarship but also across the whole range of his scholarly interests and pursuits. It is this engagement with power that can be seen as always and already embedded in Ivor's scholarship and that is implicit in every aspect of his theoretical and methodological orientation.

In his curriculum studies Ivor proved himself adept at deconstructing the circuits of power that enabled a particular (academic) tradition to maintain its stranglehold on curriculum form (Goodson, 1983). Kincheloe (1997) gets to the heart of what made this possible:

> Understanding the propensity of political students of curriculum to focus on general cultural dynamics (macro-theories) to explain educational inequality and the tendency of phenomenologically-based students to privilege the particularistic

domain of classroom interaction (micro-theories), Goodson early on recognized the need to analyze the interrelation of the two spheres of activity. (p. xv)

In other words, Ivor focuses primarily on the *dynamics* rather than the *locus* of power, using the term *mediation* to characterize the nature of this dynamic.

Importantly, because this is an embodied rather than an abstracted process, Ivor refutes analyses that see curriculum as being "handed down" by forces of domination or the sociological explanation of teacher socialization. Instead:

The evidence indicates not so much domination by dominant forces as solicitous surrender by subordinate groups. This does not indicate a process of teacher socialisation into the dominant institution so much as teachers' material self-interest in their working lives. (Goodson, 1983, p. 193)

To use everyday language, this indicates that teachers were making the most of a bad job. Teachers are not all-powerful but they do have the means to "mediate" in the terms of their surrender. Conceptualized thus the locus of power undergoes a subtle shift. A focus on the dynamics of power simultaneously offers a way to deconstruct the mechanisms by and through which ideas that operate at global and national levels come to be made operational at local levels. This in turn suggests a complex sort of empowerment for those who might otherwise be seen simply as victims or hostages to fortune, without a concomitant recourse to simplistic or overblown claims that position actors as entirely in charge of their own destinies. This insistence that both agency *and* structure *and* the relationship between them are crucial sites for the interrogation of power has continued to be a feature of Ivor's work, particularly, and I will pick up these ideas in the remaining chapters of "Reading Ivor Goodson."

The Past, Present, and Future (Social) Significance of the Study of Curriculum

We have seen that Ivor's personal biography, the history of schooling, and the influence of broader social movements formed a nexus of preoccupations and possibilities that was to lead him to a decades-long immersion in the study of curriculum. The dynamic among his pedagogic orientations, his social origins, his formative background as a historian, his work as a teacher, and his personal "lifestyle" rooted in popular and vernacular culture, in tandem with his specific location in the academy and his sense of mission, led, moreover, to a particular epistemological starting point for his studies. He was not alone in his desire to realize social justice in and through the medium of curriculum. He was not the only scholar whose experiences informed his epistemology. However, it was the particular way in which he incorporated and integrated the ideological and experiential in his approach to the study of curriculum, informed by a historical sensibility and supported methodologically by life history genres, that furnished a different ontological and theoretical basis for the study of curriculum formation, and that in turn established the foundations of an approach to understanding the mechanisms not just of schooling but of social construction in general. His scholarship emphasized the centrality of lived realities and of commonsense perspectives, but nonetheless insisted on theoretical interpellations grounded in historical recall. This marked a departure from approaches in curriculum studies that were centered either on the high ground of theory or the low ground of classroom practice and addressed omissions in philosophical and sociological approaches.

All that notwithstanding, and even though it went against his desires (Goodson, 2011, p. 40), in the early years of the 1990s Ivor had started to pay less attention to curriculum per se so that by the end of the twentieth century he was no longer engaged in the study of curriculum to any great extent. Although this cannot be construed as a retreat from the field and most certainly does not indicate a change in his core concerns or prefigurative politics, it does indicate the vibrancy of his strategic politics and their sensitivity to trends on the broader stage. Working in tandem with his moral compass, they led to recognition that an acceleration in the drive toward the marketization, and hence stratification, of schooling was repositioning the field of inquiry and squeezing out the possibility for a critical curriculum scholarship that had linkages to the wider social processes of schooling. In short, the privileging of "choice" over social inclusion was serving to reposition the field of curriculum studies as "a set of marginal arguments about inclusion and exclusion. So the big arguments are arguments about the nature of schooling and the distribution of schooling" (2011, p. 40). The diminution in his involvement with curriculum also presaged Ivor's appreciation that rapacious powers of accumulation and consumption would in the future be concentrated on subjectivity and that people's life narratives would present the means through which this would be accomplished. His turn from an intense involvement with curriculum was in anticipation of this.

That said, the pendulum swing back to curriculum that Ivor believed would occur at some point seems to be gaining some momentum. Curriculum issues are once again taking a more prominent place on the political landscape and hence in that of his scholarship (in press). This is not, however, merely the unproblematic resumption of his previous scholarship, picking up where he left off. In the first place he never entirely left off, and second, the context in which he is putting his ideas to work has changed. The rise of narrative politics (Salmon, 2010) and the narrativization of social and political processes requires curriculum to be brought into even closer proximity with personal narratives (Goodson, in press). It requires (re)thinking about how theories about narrative can be translated into tools for learning and hence for action, which in turn asks questions of learning itself (Goodson, Biesta, Tedder, & Adair, 2010) and of pedagogy (Goodson & Gill, 2011). Hence, Ivor's scholarship manifests a continuum of concerns that is nevertheless responsive to the changing landscape of their location and the desire for a just "social future" (in press) that has been at the heart of his whole scholarly career and of his "life politics" for almost the whole of his life.

This triumvirate of the persistence of his enduring concerns, an appreciation of the need to be responsive to changes on the broader sociopolitical canvas, and an engagement with life narratives and life histories as a means of confronting power in the contest for subjectivity furnishes both the overarching rationale and the underpinning foundations for the foci of his scholarship from the beginning of the 1990s, which is the subject of the next two chapters. The first looks at his engagement with the study of teachers' lives, professional knowledge, and educational reform, and this in turn serves as a bridge between Ivor's work on curriculum and his most recent involvement with narrative.

Chapter 7

Teachers' Lives, Professional Knowledge, Educational Reform

Researching teachers' lives is an enterprise fraught with danger but the alternative is, I think, more dangerous: to continue in substantial ignorance of those people who, in spite of the many historical shifts and cycles, remain central to achievement in the educational endeavour.

(Goodson, 1992c, pp. 15–16)

By the beginning of the 1990s Ivor no longer saw curriculum as a major site of contestation and he turned instead to the broad area of study that comes under the umbrella of "life politics," which I discussed in Chapter 5 and which he defines as "the politics of identity construction and ongoing identity maintenance" (Goodson, 2005a, p. 181). This chapter will attend to the way in which he addressed these issues as they pertain to educational inquiry. It deals specifically with the period that began immediately after his most intense involvement with curriculum matters until he turned more explicitly to an engagement with narrative scholarship. This, roughly, covers the years from the beginning of the 1990s until the early years of the new millennium, although there is always considerable overlap and run off when academic attention shifts from one area to another. Watertight compartmentalizing is not possible—and neither would it reflect reality, which was somewhat messier than a progression narrative can convey. That said, the beginning of the 1990s saw Ivor focusing more intently on what can broadly be described as "teachers' lives," particularly in relation to professional knowledge, educational reform, and change theory, but which was also expanded to include the lives of other public service professionals not only in the UK but also across Europe (Goodson, 2003; Goodson & Lindblad, 2011).

Three points will serve to anchor the discussion. The first is that this period of refocusing did not represent a move to pastures new, not least because from the start of his academic career Ivor insisted that teachers held the key to the success of educational enterprise and that it was therefore essential to see things from their perspective as well as from other vantage points. It was this desire to include teachers that underpins his calls to rehabilitate life history genres, and it is his sponsorship and interrogation of these genres that constitute one of the pillars of his scholarship (1980–1981). We have also seen that his seminal work on curriculum included the personal experiences of Sean Carson and his efforts to establish environmental studies as an examinable subject. Ivor's inclusion of this perspective served not only to illustrate and animate the arguments he was making, but also as a point of entry to theorizing curriculum formation in general. The publication of *Teachers' Lives and Careers* (Goodson & Ball, 1989) added further substantive concerns to these early methodological explorations and rehearsed the foundational precepts on which his subsequent study of professional lives and knowledge was built. Ivor went on to develop and refine these ideas in his later work on teachers' lives and in the related study of professional knowledge (1992c, 2003; Goodson & Hargreaves, 1996) but it is also clear that from the beginning of his career he reflexively and critically anticipated the implications, opportunities, and dangers of approaches that took teachers' lives as the departure point and referent to educational inquiry (1997b).

The second point is that this more intensive focus on life politics, which was primarily addressed through the prism of teachers' lives, is not synonymous with a break with the past, a signal that Ivor had exhausted his interest in curriculum, that he had mined this seam in the interests of his own career and was now moving on. Not only does this present a picture of Ivor that is at odds with his ethical and moral standpoint, which is implicit in the role of the public intellectual and which he often apologizes for because it makes him sound pious and "holier than thou," it is a reading that makes little sense in light of his punishing work rate since then. He could, after all, have scaled down his involvement with curriculum and traded on his reputation. It makes more sense to interpret this move as a reflection of the fact that he no longer saw curriculum as a major site for engagement with the issues that were of greatest concern to him. He therefore had to take his continuing preoccupations and relocate to a site where he believed they had greater salience.

In other words, Ivor's concerns, which manifest themselves in broad terms as a commitment to the achievement of social justice, remain constant regardless of the arenas into which he takes them. As I set out in Chapter 5, in light of the rise of postmodern sensibilities and changes on the political scene, Ivor saw the broad area of "life politics" as the place to which he needed to direct his attention. What is more, although Ivor turned down the volume on his study of curriculum, this does not signify that he had entirely cut himself off from an interest in it, or that he had no intention of returning to this site of engagement. Indeed, because he takes an Annaliste view that conceptualizes time in terms of cycles and pendulum swings, it is likely he knew that he would be returning there in due course and he continued to keep a close eye on developments (Goodson, Anstead, & Mangan, 1998; Goodson et al., 2002; Goodson & Anstead, 2010). As I set out in the previous chapter, the time to focus more closely on curriculum again seems to have arrived (Goodson, in press).

The third point that will anchor our discussion pivots on the distinction between the discrete study of teachers' life politics and educational inquiry that takes the centrality of teachers to the success or failure of educational enterprise as its starting point, inquiry that is therefore conducted through the prism of teachers' lives and that includes views from the vantage point of teachers. This is in some respects a matter of separating methodology from substantive concerns and I will approach both of these separately in this chapter. But in other respects the distinction should not be overdrawn. After all, Ivor had begun to blur the boundaries when he included teachers even in his earliest work on curriculum (Goodson, 1983). Nevertheless, it is important to recognize that concomitant with the substantive focus of the work Ivor carried out in the 1990s on professional knowledge and educational reform was his appreciation of the changes on the broader political canvas. These changes were redefining not only the way in which the work of teachers was being reinscribed but also the way in which teachers themselves were interpreting their professional lives. This had implications for how the substance of his inquiry should be approached. Therefore we must treat methodological and substantive issues in the chapter as each worthy of a discrete treatment, but at the same time due regard must be given to their dynamic because it is an understanding of the latter that gives Ivor's scholarship its distinctive flavor.

I have therefore structured the chapter in the following way. I will first give some background to the reason Ivor relocated to this area of engagement. To a great extent this will represent the theory of context to the story of action that follows. I will then set out some of the methodological and theoretical precepts that inform his approach to substantive concerns before shifting the discussion to a more discrete focus on the substantive issues in and around his study of professional knowledge and educational reform.

The Context for the Turn to Research on "Life Politics"

As the opening quotation to this chapter makes clear, Ivor has consistently argued that including teachers in educational research and in research on education is a fraught enterprise, but that it is nevertheless worth grappling with its problems because teachers are central to analysis and understanding on both descriptive and theoretical levels. I have already set out that his convictions about this contention consolidated when he met a former teacher who had been instrumental in drawing the cognitive maps (a term Ivor used in conversation with me and to which I return in the next section) that had led him from working on a production line in a crisp factory to his subsequent career as a public intellectual. Ivor knew that this teacher was committed not only to socialist principles but also to helping students, and yet he was resisting reform that would have supported both because his "centre of gravity" was no longer in school. If not exactly an epiphanic moment, because Ivor was already leaning in this direction, then the argument for including teachers' life politics, particularly when studying innovation or reform in education, was certainly reinforced during this meeting. Ivor therefore considers that a failure to include teachers leads at best to emaciated analysis and at worst to ontological breakdown and a failure to appreciate the processes that are actually being engaged. He is therefore critical of technical and managerial paradigms of education change and reform, those devoid of a consideration of the personal and emotional investments that teachers are required to make in them. That said, he also takes the view that in modernist times "this absence was not of fatal significance since personal and political projects often interlinked and sometimes merged" (Goodson, 2003, p. 67). This is no longer the case.

The severance between personal and broader sociopolitical projects is in some part traceable to the "postmodern turn" and its accompanying notions of selfhood and identity as emergent and unstable. Ivor does not entirely embrace these views, but nor does he reject them out of hand. Taking the nuanced position that is a defining feature of his scholarship, he recognized that these shifts in the dynamic between the individual and the broader sociopolitical context presented both opportunities and risks. But to capitalize on the former and mitigate the latter, it is not simply a case of uncritically including stories told by teachers, in the sense of layering or adding them in to analyses, but of treating life politics as "a major and growing site of ideological and intellectual contestation" in its own right (1997b; 2005a, p. 181). Although "identity and lived experience can themselves be used as the sites wherein and whereby we interrogate, theoretically and critically, the social world" (2005a, p. 181), identity and lived experience also require the same critical and theoretical interrogation. In other words, it is not only that teachers' lives and life politics must sit at the epicenter of analyses but that we should first situate them as stories of action in theories of context and come to antecedent understandings of what has informed those life politics.

Ivor has devoted considerable thought to the issues of "representing teachers" in educational inquiry (1997b) because at the same time as he relocated from the field of curriculum he was becoming increasingly aware that the effects and influences of economic restructuring were increasingly implicated in and were interfering with the possibilities for doing so. He sets out his thinking on these issues in his pivotal paper "The Story So Far," which he began to develop in tandem with his relocation from the arena of curriculum studies in the early 1990s and first published in the *International Journal of Qualitative Studies in Education* in the autumn of 1995; the slightly amended version of the paper that I am using here appears in the volume of his selected works (2005a, pp. 187–199).

In this paper Ivor argues that economic restructuring has pierced the "mediating membrane" of median institutions and secondary associations such as schools and the family, which had previously acted as a "buffer zone" between the individual and macro-political forces. Little stands now between "the subject/state, consumer/market confrontation" (Goodson, 2005a, p. 188). This has paved the way for a "cultural re-definition" in which "grand narratives" are displaced as cultural resources in the construction of personal narratives. Although grand narratives were not an unmitigated good and could work in exclusionary ways, they nevertheless offered access to knowledge about general patterns, social contexts, and critical theories and therefore offered access to knowledge that stood outside the individual's frame of reference (p. 188). What is more, the simultaneous dissolution of grand narratives and the privileging of personal stories cut off from access to the knowledge grand narratives enshrine is achieved through a recursive, self-referential process. Local, individualized, atomized life stories and personal anecdotes themselves are promoted to act as a reference point for the construction of our life stories.

Ivor has therefore concluded that "in the cultural logic of late capital the life story represents a form of cultural apparatus to accompany a newly aggrandizing state and market system," "a learned discourse comprising stories and practices—specific local and located but divorced from understandings of social context and social process" (Goodson, 2005a, p. 188). The inclusion of teachers' stories therefore offered "the chance for a large step forward in representing the lived experience of schooling" (p. 187) but in doing so we are potentially "sponsoring genres of inquiry in the name of empowerment, whilst at the same time, effectively disempowering the very people and causes we seek to work with" (p. 187). Ivor therefore concludes that:

> As we witness the claim that we are at "the end of history" it's perhaps unsurprising that life stories are being divorced from any sense of history, any sense of the politically and socially constructed nature of the "circumstances" in which lives are lived and meanings made. Truly "men make their own history" *but also more than ever "not in circumstances of their own choosing."* (2005a, p. 185, emphasis added)

It is against this backdrop of the methodological and theoretical issues this raises that we now need to read Ivor's work on teachers' lives.

Methodological Precepts: Life History, Not Life Story

One of the foundational precepts that can be found in *Teachers' Lives and Careers* is that educational inquiry that placed teachers at its center had to be sensitive to material difference *and* subjective experience. Although there was likely to be common ground in their experiences, the term *teachers* is not a collective noun. Teachers may be individuals together but they are individuals nonetheless. Therefore in calling for a greater focus on "teachers" Ivor drew attention to the obvious but oft overlooked fact that:

> careers are socially constructed and individually experienced over time. They are subjective trajectories through historical periods and at the same time contain their own organizing principles and distinct phases. (Goodson & Ball, 1989, p. 9)

However, this should not be taken for an un-nuanced call to "give voice" to teachers or to unreflexively or uncritically incorporate their personal experience. It is clear from the above quotation, which highlights his sensitivity to differences in subjective experiences, that Ivor's objection here was not related to the inclusion of personal stories per se. Nor was it that he feared including them might be synonymous with the production of myriad conflicting accounts. On the contrary, he welcomes and embraces complexity in scholarship because it reflects what he knows to be the complexity in life. His reservations arise precisely because he thinks this would not be likely to happen if teachers were simply given a space into which they could talk. In Ivor's view stories may be individually narrated but they are not autonomous creations. They are instead social constructions in two senses. The first is that they proceed from and embody a particular consciousness, one that is itself a product of its social, structural, and cultural location. Ivor acknowledges the way in which this idea was central to early feminist thought, expressed, for example, in the notion of "consciousness raising" as a political response to patriarchal oppressions. Second, personal stories draw on dominant, prefigurative, or prior, "scripts" in their construction.

Ivor conceptualizes prior scripts as products of our consciousness and hence indirectly of our social, structural, cultural, and historical location, but he also makes a more direct connection between our scripts and our location, in that personal stories incorporate to a greater or lesser extent the storylines that are available at any given time. These storylines embody and reflect prevailing conditions and because these conditions change, so too do storylines. Ivor often cites the script of the scholarship boy, for example. Richard Hoggart (1958) is to Ivor's mind a major inscriber of this storyline, but his work now seems outdated not because boys from working-class backgrounds no longer pass their 11-plus and go to grammar school (because they do) but because the referents to which it appeals no longer have currency. The scholarship boy storyline reflects "outmoded models of meritocracies, masculinisms, and Marxisms" (Goodson, 2005a, p. 216). Likewise, the "coming out" storyline (Plummer, 1995) was not one that was available to Oscar Wilde, for example. They are therefore stories that he sees as working in two chronological directions (Goodson, 2005a, p. 214). Reaching out to the past, they are imbued with collective memory so that they can be narrated without the need for explication. Indeed, so familiar are they that the listener can often anticipate what is coming next and a deviation from the script can create a sense of dissonance. They also provide a sense-making framework for our future actions. It is impossible to entirely sidestep the influence of these storylines. Even stories of resistance, such as Ivor's resistance to the script of the scholarship boy, are told in relation to them.

In light of this, Ivor concludes that the possibility of capturing individual voices is illusory. Indeed he questions the notion of the "personal story" because when we hear life stories, at best, "(w)hat we capture, in fact, is a mediation between the personal voice and wider cultural imperatives" (Goodson, 2005a, p. 215). At worst we could be giving voice to a celebration of scripts of domination (2003). This is one of the reasons he insists that, if life stories are to be a conduit to understanding social life, the process whereby they are employed must involve not only *narration* but also *location* and *collaboration*.

The concept of location has temporal, situational, and historical aspects in that it indicates that stories have to be set not only in the context of the time in which they are narrated, but due regard must also be given to the history of that context. It is significant, for example, that *Teachers' Lives and Careers* was written at a time when there was an assault on teachers' morale. Teachers were being blamed for a failure to adapt the curriculum in line with the changing needs of British industry and, by implication, responsibility for economic recession was also being laid at their door. This marked "both a loss of professional self-respect among teachers and a shift in public esteem for the teaching profession" (1985, p. 5), assertions that my own recollections substantiate. In contrast, *Teachers' Professional Lives* (Goodson & Hargreaves, 1996) was written at a time when setting professional standards and redefining what it means to be a professional were at the forefront of educational reform.

However, as salient as this is, Ivor argued that an analysis that proceeded from these snapshots in time alone was not sufficient. Thus, teachers' sense of betrayal that was noted in *Teachers' Lives and Careers* makes more sense if it is located historically, "within the unique fifty year period of relative autonomy granted to them by the withdrawal of the Board of Education from direct oversight of the school curriculum in the 1920s" (Goodson & Ball, 1989, p. 6). In short, by including this historical background we gain a heightened appreciation of the extent to which particular forces, both external and internal to teaching, affected teachers' sense of professional identity.

Hand in hand with the need to locate personal stories, Ivor also advocated an educational inquiry that took the form of a collaborative enterprise between teachers based in schools and researchers based in the academy, or, as Ivor construes it, between the "life story giver" and the "research taker" (Goodson, 2005a, p. 95). Although he takes a position that emphasizes the interestedness rather than the disinterestedness of the academy and recognizes that "those in the academy might take information on teachers' lives and use it entirely for their own purposes," he nevertheless believes this is a risk worth taking. Without it teachers are left with an incomplete picture of what is going on and my own experience as a teacher supports this contention. When I finally "left" teaching, at least teaching in comprehensive schools, it was with a sense of personal failure. I felt I had the "complete picture" only when reading Ivor's work as part of my doctoral research.

The danger that the power relationships between story giver and research taker might tip too far in the balance of the latter will be considerably mitigated in Ivor's view if the collaborative relationship is set up as a "fair trade" between the two. The key to this fair trade is the structural location of the parties involved:

> one of the valuable characteristics of a collaboration between teachers as researchers and external researchers is that it is a collaboration between two parties that are differentially located in structural terms. Each sees the world through a different prism of practice and thought. This valuable difference may provide the external researcher with a possibility to offer back goods in "the trade". The teacher/researcher offers data and insights. The terms of trade, in short, look favourable. In such conditions collaboration may at last begin. (Goodson & Walker, 1991, pp. 148–149)

In this sense both teacher and researcher are transformed into giver *and* taker.

Ivor's insistence on including teachers' stories, but doing so in such a way that is cognizant of their structural, cultural, temporal, and historical location, is at the heart of his sponsorship of life history genres and of his understanding of the difference between them. In short, "the life story individualizes and personalizes, the life history contextualizes and politicizes" (Goodson & Sikes, 2001, pp. 87–88). This distinction is nice enough, but its significance travels beyond its methodological parameters:

> I have often asked administrators and educational bureaucrats why they support personal and practical forms of knowledge for teachers in the form of narratives and stories. Their comments often echo those of the "true believers" in narrative method. But I always go on, after suitable pause and diversion, to ask "what do you do on your leadership courses?" There it is always "politics as usual" management skills, quality assurance, micropolitical strategies, personnel training. Personal and practical stories for some, cognitive maps of power for others. So whilst the use of stories and narratives can provide a useful breathing space away from power it does not suspend the continuing administration of power; indeed it could well make this so much easier. (Goodson, 1997b, p. 116)

In other words, the inclusion of unmediated life stories has the potential to fortify centers of power while simultaneously inscribing life stories as marginal, the old game of divide and rule (2005a, p. 199). Contextualized life histories can potentially mitigate this process by building a bridge between the personal significance of stories to their sociopolitical functions. It is precisely that these sociopolitical functions are now serving to privilege atomized, individualized, private stories that has given Ivor pause for thought.

Theoretical Precepts: Middle Ground Theorizing

Ivor's concerns about the promotion of genres of "personal, practical experience" have implications not only for methodological approaches but also for theory building. In most Western countries there has been a move away from foundational disciplinary theories in educational studies in recent decades because they are seen as being too far removed from the practical world of the teacher and of little relevance to them. There has been a concomitant desire to reenter the teacher's world (Goodson, 2008, p. vii). Ivor is critical of theories that disenfranchise teachers. Nor is he convinced by theories of domination that, even if they do not entirely deny individual agency, position it as always and already ineffectual. But, as we have seen, he is equally critical of the unmediated inclusion of "personal, practical experience" because it can serve to reinforce the power imbalances it seeks to dismantle:

> Sole reliance on narrative becomes a convenient form of political quietism—we can continue telling our stories (whether as life "stories" or research "stories") and our searchlight never shines on the social and political construction of lives and life circumstances. (2005a, p. 185)

He argues instead for theories of power that recognize the way in which individuals mediate the effects of macro-political forces in their daily lives because on these terms the individual is always and already actively engaged with power.

In short, Ivor is not wholly dismissive either of foundational disciplinary theory or of the inclusion of personal experience, but nor does he consider either as a sufficient basis for theorizing. He doubts the power of either, on their own, to expand our understanding and he criticizes each for their omission of the historical context in which they both are situated. He advocates:

> developing theory in the "middle ground": the arena between structural organization and policy of political contexts and the micro-detail of daily life in classrooms and teaching. . . . Middle ground theory seeks to combine the view from below with a focus on strategies and organizational forms that respond to changes in micro-level organizational structure and policy contexts. (2008, p. vii)

Ivor is not advocating compromise—neither structural organization nor the micro-politics of daily life stands to lose anything here. Instead he is clearing a new space for theory at the interface of the personal and the political.

Occupying the middle ground and working at this interface has several advantages in Ivor's view:

> By focusing on the middle ground substantive theories at that level can produce connections with daily teaching realities and—facing the other way—with formal theories of a structuralist and post-structuralist kind. (Goodson, 2008, p. vii)

Tracing these connections means, for example, that we are also able to see what happens "on the ground" to policies that are passed down from "above" and we can also locate our analyses at different points and intersections along those directional axes. This in turn enables us to take account of temporal and historical factors. For instance, Ivor has noted how at different junctures teachers have been characterized as "villains," "victims," or even dupes of the system within which they were required to operate (Goodson & Ball, 1989, p. 7; Goodson, 2008, p. 2). Whichever characterization has currency at the time will then have implications for how teachers see their life and work. Whether it is devoid of overarching understandings about how and why these characterizations have currency, or of teachers' personal experience of being positioned thus, omitting either truncates the possibilities of both. If the structural element is omitted we miss the opportunity to locate the teachers' experience as politically and socially constructed. If personal experience is omitted we have not "confronted the complexity of the school teacher as an active agent making his or her own history" (2008, p. 2).

In some respects this is simply the call for the inclusion of life politics, but it also encompasses such things as commonly understood life stages that are also but not exclusively linked to the processes of aging. Having children affected greatly my career not only materially but also in terms of the evolution of my identity as a teacher, for example, and any teacher knows the blessings and curses of being close, or far, in age to those they are teaching. It includes their previous career history and the life experiences that shape their view of teaching and the way they approach it. It factors in their lives outside school, their latent identities, and their structural and cultural location. Teachers' professional lives must be seen to be in a dynamic with all other aspects of their life across and for the duration of their lives.

Substantive Applications: Professional Knowledge, Professional Lives, and Educational Reform

I will now flesh out the methodological and theoretical imperatives of researching teachers' lives that I have set out in a disembodied way earlier by outlining how they were applied to and how they manifested themselves in Ivor's research into changing ideas about professional knowledge and professional lives in the context of policy discourses about educational reform. There are a number of different ways in which one might approach this topic, not least through a consideration of Ivor's work into the way in which educational restructuring across Europe is being "refracted" by teachers and by the teaching profession, rather than being received and implemented in a uniform way (Goodson & Lindblad, 2011). Refraction is a core idea in Ivor's thinking. It expresses the way in which and the degree to which educational reforms are taken up (or resisted and rejected) and how they are subject to a matrix of factors that depend on historical periodization and the trajectory of social engagement of the countries concerned. It undermines the notion that reform can be delivered in a top-down way that ignores these factors. Ivor contrasts the situation in Finland and Sweden where "deeply entrenched systems of social democracy and professional expertise appear to be enduring" (p. 106) with that in Spain, Portugal, and Greece, whose systems of social welfare and democracy are relatively young. "Hence the restructuring world movement enters these societies at a different stage, and so to speak, at a different angle" (p. 106).

However, I have chosen to focus more closely here on a paper titled "All the Lonely People: The Struggle for Private Meaning and Public Purpose in Education" (Goodson, 2007) because it instantiates all the key points that I raised in the earlier sections on methodology, theory, and the changing meaning of the contextual location of personal stories. It gets to the heart of Ivor's thinking about the meaning of professionalism as well as addressing the substantive implications of delivering "top down" reform that fails to pay due regard to teachers' professional knowledge (and indeed those of other public service professionals). The notion of "professionalism" with regard to teachers is not easy to define, not least because teachers themselves have in the past been unclear about whether they are professionals or cultural workers (Goodson & Hargreaves, 1996). Nevertheless, Ivor was critical of reforms that aimed to "raise professional standards" in schools but that failed to incorporate an awareness of the "the way in which people conduct their professional lives and generate, thereby, professional and personal meanings and missions" (Goodson, 2007, p. 132):

> In very few instances have school reforms or change theories been promulgated which place personal development and change as central "building blocks" in the process. Instead, changes have been pursued in ways that seem to insist this will happen, in spite of the teacher's personal beliefs and missions. All too often, the "personality of change" has been seen as the "stumbling block" of real reform, rather than as a crucial "building block." (2007, p. 138)

Immanent in this call for recognition of the "personality of change," therefore, is the necessity of paying due regard to the interplay of the personal and the political.

The catalyst for much of Ivor's thinking on the implications of this failure occurred when he was conducting research for a project funded by the Spencer Foundation that investigated "change over time" in schools in Canada and the United States. For Ivor the forms of knowledge we produce is closely allied to our identities and to the perceptions we have of ourselves, and therefore part of the changes investigated related to this. The research was undertaken using life history methodologies and interviews were carried out with three cohorts of teachers whose service spanned five decades from the 1950s. In the course of this research, during what he terms an "epiphanic moment" (Goodson, 2007, p. 133), Ivor realized that the way in which teachers perceived their roles had changed over time. Older teachers spoke of a sense of vocationalism and of dedication to the job. But for younger cohorts, teachers in the new millennium, their sense of mission and purpose in life lay elsewhere, in the plans and projects they had out of school.

This is significant in itself but it takes on heightened meaning when considered in light of its implications. Reforms that were supposed to "raise standards" in teaching, by ridding the profession of those "old professionals" who had in the past enjoyed a certain degree of professional autonomy and replacing them with "technicians who follow government guidelines and teach a curriculum which is prescribed by governments or departments of education" (2007, p. 146), have instead served to eradicate a sense of committed professionalism.

Ivor considers the implications of a profession divested of "old professionals," those who "(view) the work of teaching as comprising more than material reward and technical delivery, as a form of work overlaid with purpose, passion and meaning" (Goodson, 2007, p. 139), a profession that is populated instead with the demoralized and those who regard teaching as "just a job." He groups these implications under the headings of "memory loss," "mentoring loss," and "retention and recruitment." Memory loss refers to the loss of professional knowledge when "the more mature members of an industry are given early retirement or subjected to change and reform they disagree with." Mentoring loss refers to a break in the "chain of transmission" of professional knowledge, either because "old professionals" who are disenchanted with reform keep knowledge to themselves or because younger cohorts are not sufficiently interested in gaining this knowledge. In terms of recruitment, it seems that a "putting off" of the old professionals has led to a "turning off" of younger cohorts. Schools are struggling to recruit. Likewise, they are not committing to teaching as a long-term occupation but as a stepping stone to the realization of other dreams and missions.

Ivor emphasizes the implications of these points with reference to the changes in the railways in the UK where "clever technology" had replaced experienced railway workers and was literally found fatally wanting. Although bad teaching is hardly a killer, memory loss in teaching might be seen as equally serious in its ramifications for the education of current and future generations. And while these ideas are expressive in themselves, their significance reaches even further in the way they signal a change in attitudes to public life and public service in general:

> the new world order is in profound danger of "losing the battle for the hearts and minds" of its own citizens, certainly in the struggle to deliver better public services and a reinvigorated public life. (2007, p. 133)

Chapter 8

Narrative

Are stories too egalitarian, too inclusive, for an educational system that seeks to select and foster certain groups but not others?

(Goodson, 2013, p. 4)

Before turning the spotlight on Ivor's narrative scholarship itself, two points will serve by way of orientation. First, my treatment of it in this chapter reflects understandings that were formed during a "pedagogic encounter" with him that took the form of a conversation about aspects of his scholarship. This encounter will form the backbone of the next section on "Teaching Ivor Goodson." In this sense this chapter does three things: it eases our transition from a focus on substantive issues to one that is orientated more toward methodological questions; it animates the central tenets of Ivor's thinking on narrative pedagogy; and it instantiates the outcome of a particular narrative process advocated by him, namely the creation of a "third voice" that arises during such pedagogic encounters. Second, to avoid overrepetition of any one phrase, I refer to Ivor's research and scholarship *on, into,* and *about* narrative (and narration) in a number of ways. Although he has used life history methodologically for his research into narrative, I am not alluding here to the suite of approaches that constitute narrative research as such.

There are three overlapping and interwoven strands to Ivor's study of narrative: development of theories of narrative (Goodson, 2013); investigation of the forms and applications of narrative learning (Goodson et al., 2010); and the possibilities and practices of narrative pedagogy (Goodson & Gill, 2011). These foci indicate that in one respect his narrative research represents his *re*turn to those areas of learning and pedagogy that informed his study of curriculum, rather than his entry into a completely new field, and indeed it marks the beginning of his return to curriculum issues themselves (Goodson, in press). That said, I have emphasized throughout this reading of his work that when his focus changes it is not a sign that his interests and concerns and preoccupations have changed. In the sense that there are some unwavering constants in his life/work he embodies the Goodson family motto that they are "a very persistent family." Changes in the direction of his gaze signify instead that the sites on which they are being contested have changed. Ivor's involvement with narrative indicates therefore that he now sees it as a site on which important social and political battles are being fought. Because "to a large extent the stories about our lives and ourselves *are* who we are" (Biesta, Field, Hodkinson, Macleod, & Goodson, 2011, p. 51, original emphasis), Ivor comprehends that the battle now being fought on the site of narrative is over subjectivity itself, a point that I will elucidate presently.

Ivor's turn to narrative, then, represents a *re*turn rather than a fresh departure, the continuation of his life/work and an engagement with his enduring preoccupations on a different site of contestation. That being the case, I will first set out what these preoccupations are. They will by now be familiar and I have given an account of all of them over preceding chapters. Nevertheless, specifying them again provides the necessary background and context for understanding not only the focus of his study of narrative but also its motivation, as an engagement with the implications for subjectivity and selfhood wrought by the shifts and changes on the broader sociopolitical, socioeconomic, and cultural landscape. I will then look at the salient features of his work on narrative that cluster around ideas about narrative character and narrative capacity, which in turn inform the development of theories of narrative. Finally, I attend to the application of those narrative theories to learning and pedagogy, which in the context of his motivations for study can be framed as preparation for and a response to the battle over subjectivity.

Enduring Concerns . . .

In one respect Ivor's study of narrative seems an obvious one. His attachment to stories can be traced back to growing up in a family that privileged oral storytelling traditions over literary modes of cultural transmission. Storytelling is visceral for Ivor. It is in his heart and in his blood and as he has also held on to old attachments and tenaciously pursued answers to questions he first asked as a child, it seems inevitable that he would at some point focus more closely on stories. However, even though he can be romantic and nostalgic, we have seen that Ivor is also strategic. His mission is to work as a public intellectual in the achievement of a more just society for tribes like his own whose possibilities are currently circumscribed. Therefore, as attached as he is to stories, he has taken pains to embed them in and connect them to their location in broader social, political, cultural, and historical landscapes. This he has done methodologically through his sponsorship of life history genres and theoretically by situating theory building on the middle ground, where, to draw on Mills (1959), the processes of exchange between and transformations of public issues and personal troubles can be delineated and harnessed in the service of greater understanding. He brings all these commitments to his study of narrative.

Like Polkinghorne (1995) Ivor believes it is their organization around and along a central plot that distinguishes narratives from stories and to this he also adds his ideas that "personal" life stories are in fact social constructions. Not only do stories reflect and embody a particular consciousness, one that is itself a product of its social, structural, and cultural location, they also draw on dominant, prefigurative, or prior "scripts" and storylines in their construction. He cites the script of the scholarship boy in relation to his own story to illustrate that even if we construct our own narratives as a story of resistance, we do not escape from the structuring influences of these prefigurative scripts. Therefore Ivor does not hold that stories are unique creations, unencumbered by external influences. Instead he agrees with Booker (2006) that there are a finite number of plots and storylines that characterize our life stories so that while they are subjective, they are far from idiosyncratic. This idea has also been supported empirically, by Frank (1995) for example, who identified three archetypal storylines in his study of illness and disability.

Ivor has transposed this line of thinking about stories to his study of narrative, but he has done so for a particular reason. In the previous chapter I pointed out that at the start of the 1990s Ivor proved himself remarkably perceptive in anticipating the cultural implications of economic restructuring. In particular, in "The Story So Far" (2005a, pp. 185–199), he set out how this had affected cultural understandings and how this "cultural redefinition" was serving to dismantle the grand narratives that, as problematic and exclusionary as they also were, gave us access to ideas, to patterns of social life, and to social theories beyond our own individualized frames of reference. To illustrate his argument Ivor looks to music and film and to the media because he regards these genres as ahead of developments in academic circles and hence can act as harbingers of things to come. His reference to the trajectory of the work of Bruce Springsteen, whom he regards as a particularly perceptive social storyteller, struck a particular chord with me because for years I had been a massive fan of his. A framed poster of his "Born in the USA" tour of 1984–1985 hung in my kitchen until 1998. And yet in recent years, without even being aware of it, I had stopped listening to his output. Ivor's analysis clarified the reasons for this transformation in my allegiance. In short, Springsteen's original concerns with the everyday accommodations of the individual (largely men, it must be said) within the context of changing circumstances, particularly de-industrialization and changing patterns of employment, have likewise been transformed. His concerns are now with the impact of the "risky" times in which we live on the *souls,* arguably the ultimate site of interiority, of those individuals.

. . . On New Sites of Contestation

I have so far set out the way in which Ivor has entered the field of inquiry into narrative and this also serves to provide a basis for understanding why he has relocated his concerns into this particular arena. At this point it is important to make a distinction between Springsteen's retreat into interiority and Ivor's involvement in the inner workings of stories. By relocating his existing preoccupations to the site of narrative, Ivor is signaling that his project is not to work *with* the transformations in social life but to work *against* them by *critically* engaging with them and thereby to provide an effective response to them. But this requires two things. One is to understand what narratives are, to get to grips with their mechanisms and their inner processes and to develop theories of narrative. The other is to understand the nature of the sociopolitical transformations in which this work is being carried out and the way in which this affects the nature of narrative. This articulates the demand to situate stories of action within theories of context and, before we attend to Ivor's study of narrative per se, we need first to come to an understanding of the constituent characteristics of its wider contextual location and of their significance for Ivor's narrative work.

In the previous chapter I discussed the significance of Ivor's prediction that the grand narratives on which we could previously draw and that informed the "scripted resources" for our personal narratives would increasingly be replaced by atomized, self-referential stories that are then recursively privileged and valorized. I related that he foresaw how the diminution of scripted resources for the emplotment of personal narratives would lead to impoverished storylines and to proscribed possibilities for empowerment because it obscures the fact that "capital has historically been the vehicle for the very construction and silencing of . . . oppressed groups" (Goodson, 2005a, p. 199). He also envisaged that stories ignorant of their linkages to their wider societal and cultural positionings and their historical antecedents were not only susceptible to reinforcing old centers of power but also vulnerable to appropriation and exploitation by those centers of power, which now are specifically located in the arena of global capital.

Revisiting these ideas in "The Rise of the Life Narrative" (2006), it is clear that Ivor's insights were to a great extent prophetic. If anything he concludes that the rise of the phenomenon of "narrative politics," manifested to a great extent in the concept of "spin," whereby it is not events that count per se but the story that is told about them (Salmon, 2010, cited in Goodson, 2013, p. 13), marks a more extensive and incisive shift, that is, the narrativization of sociopolitical life itself. The ramifications of this can be traced along several axes. There are, first, implications for stories themselves, for the way they are interpreted and how their *meaning* is constructed. For example, if as Christopher Caldwell argues (2005, cited in Goodson, 2013, p. 13), politics that were once focused on capital and labor now focus instead on matters of identity and sovereignty, then stories of individual triumph are likely to be privileged over tales of collective struggle. The implications of this become clear if we apply it to the script of the scholarship boy, which will be read *and* employed differently in a context that privileges personal identity politics over commitments to social cohesion. This in turn serves to redefine the processes of and possibilities for the contextualization of personal stories.

It also has implications for the exercise of power that can now be achieved through ontological breakdown:

> Once this trick is pulled off the story can rise above material reality. So bankers can create a seismic economic collapse, but because similar groups also control the storyline which emerges, this crisis can be "restoried" as a crisis in the public sector. Economic and political control allows narrative levitation and the promotion of stories as reality. (2013, p. 13)

Substituting material reality with the hyper-real, grand narratives with personal stories, shared and collective action with individual triumphalism, and the "tyranny of the local" (David Harvey, quoted in Goodson, 2005a, p. 188) also leaves the way clear to establish new circuits of power that serve the interest of global forces, especially global capital, in the battle over subjectivity. Stories have long, probably always, been susceptible to appropriation. Carolyn Steedman (2000), for example, provides a trenchant example in her research on the Old Poor Law in England, which showed that, to qualify for relief as "deserving poor," claimants were *forced* into a particular kind of self-narration. However, these forces can now control both the scripted resources and their ontological foundations, and in so doing proscribe the possibilities for resistance by decoupling narratives from attachments to broader social projects and indeed from reality itself. Ivor therefore highlights a situation in which the narrativization of social and political life produces a proliferation and privileging of "small stories" at the same time as the separation of personal stories from their collective contexts produces a diminution in their narrative capacity (Goodson, 2006). The reach of global forces becomes both more extensive and more incisive—reaching into the most intimate spheres of our lives (Berlant, 1997).

Insofar as Ivor is committed to serving as a public intellectual, contemplating these implications acts as a catalyst for his engagement in this sphere. In some respects it represents further and continued engagement with the relationship between structure and agency that has underpinned Ivor's interrogation and use of life history genres. However, it also indicates that narrative has become a battleground for the shape, direction, and control of subjectivity. Ivor's work in the field of narrative reflects his concern to understand the nature and character of life narratives precisely because this knowledge might then be used not only to resist the assault on subjectivity outlined earlier, but also more positively to inform narrative pedagogies and enhance narrative learning. But the two aims are related. We can therefore read Ivor's move into narrative, his delving into the internal mechanisms of stories, as a shift from *charting* the ways in which narrative can function in this way, to *scrutinizing how* and *why* this might be accomplished. In other words, Ivor is concerned to investigate not only narrative character but also narrative capacity. It is to his work in this area that we shall now turn.

Toward Narrative Theory

There is an important caveat to the following discussion of Ivor's research on narrative. While he has been researching in this area since 2004, in terms of duration his full immersion in it has been relatively short-lived, certainly when we compare it to his engagement with curriculum. Although his published work on both its empirical and theoretical aspects is already formidable, the clue to its unfolding nature can be detected in the title of his book *Developing Narrative Theory* (Goodson, 2013). We apprehend him therefore while his thinking around the issues is still in process.

Ivor has come to his research on narrative with understandings gleaned from years of engaging with life history genres. Although he does credit personal life stories with the ability to re-present aspects of our lives and our selves, he also understands that the relationship between the two is complicated, and he regards life and self as both object and outcome of stories. His scholarship has, moreover, led him to regard personal life stories as altogether more than freestanding expressions of personal beliefs and preferences. They are instead particular examples of a relationship between social structures and agency. To reiterate, social structures provide "scripts" or "scripted resources," particular storylines around which people can construct their life stories and hence their agency. Our stories always represent "socially sanctioned" ways of telling a life story, and that is true whether the ensuing available storylines are embraced or resisted. The nature and meaning of the structures that give rise to these storylines are, moreover, not static. Ivor notes how the script of the "scholarship boy" that was told in the 1950s and 1960s "served to underwrite and support a particular moment in history and a particular vision of social opportunity and social structure" (Goodson, 2013, p. 5). But independent of their historical location and regardless of their specific orientation, scripts always favor some while silencing others (p. 5).

Given their obvious importance, Ivor welcomed the opportunity to delve further into understanding how, why, and to what extent scripts work in individual lives. He was seeking answers to questions about how narratives are translated into plans of action in the real world; whether different kinds of narrativity affect our identity and agency in different ways; whether certain kinds of narratives flourish more than others in particular historical periods; and why "some people spend so much time in interior thought and self-conversation about their life story whilst others seem far less concerned and are willing to accept an externally generated script" (Goodson, 2013, p. 7). The question that cuts across all of these is fundamentally whether narrativity is a "crucial variable between external structure and personal agency" (2013, p. 7). In Ivor's view we go a long way to finding the answers to some of these questions by scrutinizing story lines.

The research that Ivor, in collaboration with other colleagues, undertook for a project on "learning lives" (Biesta et al., 2011) was particularly invaluable for this undertaking and produced a "unique archive of just how people understand and narrate their life stories" (p. 8). This archive assisted Ivor in further developing his skeptical stance in relation to the view that all stories are singular, independent of the influence of external social, political, and cultural forces and of the particular times in which they are constructed and narrated. He also concluded that three broad characteristics could be applied in the analyses of the narrative *quality* of all life stories (Biesta et al., 2011, pp. 53–54; Goodson et al., 2010).

The first of these is "narrative intensity," which covers not only the length of the story and the number of words used to tell it but also the amount of depth and detail it contains. Stories will be more or less elaborate in this respect. The second is whether a story veers more toward description or toward analysis and evaluation, whether there is an attempt to make sense of it and hence of the life. The third is related to plot and emplotment and the organizing structure of the story. He concluded, like Booker (2006), that "(f)ar from being impossibly variegated, our life stories seem to cluster into a small number of 'archetypical' plots" (Goodson, 2013, p. 63). Plots are also important in that they can be taken as evidence of learning, because they potentially indicate the degree to which the narrator has come to understand her or his life. Two further characteristics were identified that were applicable only to some of the stories, not to all of them. Although most stories were recounted chronologically, which suggests this is a dominant genre of life story in the West at this point in time, some were narrated in a thematic way. Finally, some narratives lean more toward a theorized account of life and/or self and some toward a vernacular account. In addition to their characteristics he also attended to narrative efficacy, or what people do with their stories and how their narratives could lead to "plans of action in the real world." He makes the distinction here between their learning potential or the extent to which people are able to learn from their stories and their action potential, which concerns the extent to which learning then translates into action.

The findings generated by his research into narratives and learning have painted a picture of great subtlety and complexity, which undermines ideas about direct correlations and speaks against a deterministic view of storying and storytelling. For example, although it went against initial researcher expectations it was found that:

> high narrative intensity, much analysis and a strong emplotment are not in themselves a guarantee for efficacy as not all such narratives translate into learning, nor does all narrative learning translate into action. (Biesta et al., 2011, p. 55)

A clear example of this can be found in the lives of those who become "caught" in their stories, reiterating the same plot without capitalizing on it either for learning or for action (Goodson et al., 2010). It also seems that much depends on the flexibility of the narrative to adapt to changing circumstances and on the strength of attachment by the narrator to the particular scripts that describe the narrative.

However, this should not be mistaken for a view that greater narrative flexibility equates to a better developed sense of agency or that agency might be employed in a more efficacious way. In other words, "agency should not simply be equated with the ability to adapt to changing environmental conditions. Agency can also be achieved by resisting such adaptation" (Goodson et al., 2010, p. 14). And in this respect we have returned to our starting point. Addressing the question "why narrative and why now?" involved appreciating the importance, indeed the urgency, of understanding the contextual aspects of narratives, of coming to theories of how narrative works, and of identifying its mechanisms, processes, and functions.

The vital importance of this work resides in the fact that the contexts in which our personal life narratives are situated and that furnish their scripted resources are undergoing the transformations I set out earlier. This in turn is affecting not only life stories but also the power dynamics of their relationship. When the context in question comprises the narrativization of social and political life by external, global forces of oppression, serious questions about the degree to which we might retain and exercise our agency and even our humanity come to the fore. In his work on narrative Ivor is addressing these questions by considering the application of what he has learned about narrative character and narrative capacity to learning and pedagogy. In this respect he has come back to his initial point of departure as an educational researcher, as it has also acted as a springboard to further thinking on matters of curriculum (Goodson, in press).

Narrative Learning

In the course of his research into narrative learning Ivor became increasingly interested in how people learn from their lives, in the significance of this learning for their lives, and its impact on how they actually lead their lives.

He wanted to find out if certain kinds of narrative are more suitable for the promotion of such learning, what role learning played in life (Goodson et al., 2010), and how narrative learning becomes translated into action. Narrative learning therefore refers to learning from our lives through the act of storying. This does not mean that Ivor is advocating that people *should* learn from their lives:

> We have clear evidence that people can live good, happy, rewarding lives without learning, without stories and without narrative learning. We might therefore compare the stories people tell about their lives to tools—tools people can use to learn from their lives. The focus of our analysis can thus be said to be on the qualities and characteristics of these tools as we aim to understand the relationship between narrative the narrative quality of life stories and their potential to generate learning and facilitate action. (Biesta et al., 2011, p. 52)

Moreover, there is also evidence to suggest that even when people learn from their life stories, this does not automatically mean that they are able to use this in practical ways to make changes or to consolidate what they have learned through action.

On one reading, narrative learning in this context is connected with the notion of "becoming" and can therefore be conceived of as an identity project. He does not reject the postmodern notion of the non-unitary self, and, in his concept of narrative learning as "becomingness," he embraces the idea of the emergent self. He states nevertheless that "I see identity as keeping *a meaningful narrative going*" (Goodson, 2011, p. 48, emphasis added) and that this is a project that ends only with death (Biesta et al., 2011, p. 50). In this respect Ivor recounts (from memory) a conversation he had with the playwright Arthur Miller when the latter was in his late 80s. Ivor states that Miller's account of days still spent writing was "generative" for him because:

> it pinpointed the importance of variegations or differentiations in narrative constructions as well as personal orientations. His generation's experience of old age for the great majority followed the conventional script of old age—partly daytime TV and a comfy armchair—but because of his history of narrative becoming Miller's experience was utterly different. Of course these differences involve a range of other factors beyond narrativity—health being an obvious one—but they point up how a narrative trajectory and habit of "becomingness" can support a very different experience of old age. (Goodson, 2013, p. 64)

This quotation encapsulates the basic tenets of Ivor's conceptualization of narrative learning: that such learning is important for ongoing identity formation and maintenance; that it is in a complex dynamic with contextual and mediating factors (such as prior experience and material realities); that it is neither wholly independent nor simply a product of external factors; and that it is not uniform within or between individual trajectories.

The social aspects of narrative learning are crucial to understanding its function. Pat Sikes (1997) argues that stories are a fundamental form of human communication, letting us know that "we are not alone, that other people have gone through the same things and have felt like we have" (p. 23). This means the connections made between our stories and those of others enhance our capacity to learn from them. Therefore, the conversation with Arthur Miller referred to earlier, which brought the notion of "becomingness" and the way in which it is differently realized to Ivor's scholarly attention, was afforded greater salience by the fact that Ivor's mother "was a very instructive model of becomingness" from whom he "learnt a good deal . . . about this particular narrative trajectory" (Goodson, 2013, p. 64). This in turn had personal resonance for me as I recalled my 81-year-old mother, a resident in a rehabilitation center after a stroke, complaining that the place was too full of old people with whom she had nothing in common (and she used rather more colorful language to express her displeasure). The connection that is thus forged between Arthur Miller and myself, via my mother and Ivor and his mother, amplifies the resonances of narrative learning.

I would also venture to say that this notion of learning as becomingness has personal resonance for Ivor, too, as he reflects on notions of his own becoming(ness). This in turn has two aspects to it. The first is connected to his experiences of getting older. I must emphasize that this is purely my own interpretation, proceeding from the previous two points and from my "narrative encounter" with Ivor to which I referred earlier and to which I return in the next section. My own experiences of getting older, not least my increasing difficulty in recalling names, which is causing me great distress, the accompanying accommodations in my sense of self, and my own grappling with the significance of the aging process in my own "becomingness" are also influential here. The second has a longer history. While he retains a fierce love and loyalty to the tribe of his origin, he has lived outside this milieu for more years than he lived inside it and, in conversation with him, I became aware (again, because I am in a similar position) that accommodating this aspect of his life story is still "in process," still part of the process of his narrative learning.

Another vital aspect of Ivor's understanding of narrative learning is the importance of life history. The aim of life history in this regard is to give "retrospective understanding of learning biography" (Biesta et al., 2011, p. 5). In the same way that personal resonances and social connections served to consolidate and reinforce narrative learning, so too does cognizance of its location on the broader landscape:

> When people go through those gears in terms of their own learning, when they begin to understand that they are part of the common stream of humanity, that their dilemmas are, in fact, general dilemmas confronting everyone, and they can connect therefore to bigger meta-narratives and bigger concerns, that's when they move out of the prison of selfhood into a broader plateau of concerns—and that's learning, very profound learning. (Goodson & Gill, 2011, p. 67)

Narrative Pedagogy

Separating pedagogy from learning is to a great extent a futile exercise because they articulate the same ideas from different vantage points. The distinction in the perspective here centers on the ambitions Ivor has for narrative pedagogy, namely as a way of reinvigorated ideas about curriculum (Goodson, in press). It can do so primarily through its reconfiguration of the issue of educational engagement. The issue of how to engage learners in their own learning has been a running sore in the history of schooling, certainly the history of schooling in the UK. Ivor has tackled this issue personally when working as a teacher in comprehensive schools, and in a scholarly capacity through his curriculum scholarship. He is critical of Curriculum as Prescription (CAP), based on a cognitive model of learning, because it fails to take into account the specificities of learners' lives and learning becomes a task external to the actual interests of the learner (Goodson, in press; Goodson & Deakin Crick, 2009). Drawing on Bateson's (1972) notion of "tertiary learning," Ivor proposes instead the kind of learning which "is about living without habits and routinised learning; about breaking away from predigested prescriptions of curriculum and moving to the definition, ownership and ongoing narration of our own curriculum" (Goodson & Deakin Crick, 2009, p. 226). He sees the potential of narrative pedagogy to be:

> an open-ended, facilitative pedagogy in which power relations between learner and teacher change from that of expert–novice to facilitator–learning agent. The process is formative, and builds from the life narrative of the learner. The curriculum becomes a "narratable pathway" towards the formation of identity and agency when "knowing as storying" is valued, promoted and represented. Narratives provide and create space for "pedagogic moments" [Goodson 2005a] in which people can connect with themselves, each other, their own culture and tradition, their hopes and aspirations, and ultimately with an intentional, mentored construction of knowledge which serves their personal and public trajectories. This kind of narrative learning will provide an alternative to the prescriptive learning of curricula that have disengaged generations of learners. (Goodson & Deakin Crick, 2009, p. 235)

This narrative model does not obviate the need for locating individual stories in their collective contexts but, on the contrary, insists on inclusion of these contexts as part of the pedagogical approach to narrative learning.

Here Ivor makes connection with life history methodologies in that he calls for collaboration or "intentional, mentored construction of knowledge" and the location of individual stories in their broader contexts. He outlines a pedagogy based on five stages of narrative encounter: narration, collaboration, location, theorization, and direction, adding that:

> [t]he process contains a spiral of construction and reconstruction in a cycle of narration, collaboration and location which also consists of theorisation and integration. . . . The sequences form a spiral which is a continual and ongoing intense process. (Goodson & Gill, 2005, p. 125)

Narrative exchange is the precondition of this collaborative narrative; "both parties can exchange views, vernacular theories, patterns of explanation, and in doing so, arrive at a new understanding—mutually negotiated—of the social, cultural and historical 'location' of the narrative" (Goodson & Gill, p. 42). This is a narrative pedagogy that not only restores the social *function* of narratives (inclusive curricula) but that also restores the connection of narrative with its social *setting*. Narrative pedagogy thus educates for "a new narrative transformed by historical understanding and enhanced social imagination" (p. 41).

Concluding Remarks

To summarize, it is in the contemporary conditions of the narrativization of public and private life; the destabilization of political, social, and other macro and structural contextualizing forces; and the reconfiguration of structure and agency (and the relationship between them) that we can locate Ivor's turn to the development of narrative theories. His focus on the processes of narration, his attempts to chart and understand the various aspects of narrative character, his reentry to the fields of pedagogy and learning, and his continued grappling with issues of identity all represent his belief that the most significant battle currently being fought is that over narrative control in the development of subjectivities. His narrative scholarship might reflect the same mission—for social justice, for inclusion, and for the salience of humanity—that has been detectable throughout his career. But the transposition of long-held beliefs and values to this particular field of study also articulates his awareness that the strategic response to these forces will require deeper and more extensive understanding of the processes, functions, and settings of narrative.

Hence, the focus on narrative represents here not a diminution of the scale of his ambitions, a shrinking of the scope of his scholarly and political aspirations, or a desertion of his commitment to serve as a public intellectual. On the contrary, I do not think it is to overstate the case to contend that his immersion in research on narrativity and narration signifies his belief that if we do not understand how narrative works we are going unarmed into a battle in which our humanity may be at stake. It is against the backdrop of this overarching, not to say overwhelming, concern that a discussion of Ivor's empirical and theoretical work on the inner workings of narrative must be set if its import and impetus as well as its intellectual contribution are to be appreciated.

Having now come back to where Ivor started, I see this as a fitting place from which to relocate to "Teaching Ivor Goodson." This move should not be construed as entirely independent of what has been discussed in the chapters so far. The understandings and interpretations that constitute the backbone of "Reading Ivor Goodson" will continue to serve in this capacity, but will, among other things, be animated, observed from a different angle, layered with further meanings, and slanted more explicitly toward methodological issues.

Section 2. Teaching Ivor Goodson

Chapter 9

Preamble

At the moment I do write a lot, but I least trust that. What I do trust, is the word, the delivered—what we are doing now, talking to each other. Eye contact, word—that is what I love.

(Goodson, 2011, p. 6)

I will be approaching the task of "Teaching Ivor Goodson" from three different directions—biography, scholarship, and learning and pedagogy—but the starting point for all three is a "pedagogic encounter" with Ivor that took place in his office at the University of Brighton on a dank October day in 2012. I will come back to the reasons for taking these particular approaches shortly, but first it is important to give some background to this meeting because it had a particular purpose, of a different order to that of our first meeting, which I detail in the Introduction. I had by the time of our second meeting read and reread a sizeable proportion of Ivor's output and had written much of "Reading Ivor Goodson." I was therefore anxious to discuss aspects of my interpretations with him, face to face. The conceptual lens I took to the reading is, after all, my own invention, and I wanted to get a sense of how Ivor felt about this. He had always been eager and interested to read what I had written but had refrained from commentary. His restraint had on the one hand been reassuring and confidence inspiring, but on the other I wanted to ascertain for myself that I had not been misrepresenting his position. There are things that can only be "read off the body" and that will augment, or contradict, that which is articulated verbally.

Ivor lays great store by this kind of "embodied" scholarship and at one point suggested I might include a chapter about *meeting* Ivor Goodson (personal communication, May 2012). For various reasons, I have not been able to incorporate his suggestion in quite this way, but the idea that our actions and our purposes *are* embodied nevertheless sits at the heart of the approach I am taking now to "Teaching Ivor Goodson." Academic writing often offers a purged and sanitized version of embodied communication and, in so doing, it hides the extent to which the way we look, dress, speak, and move bears upon how we are received in the world and on our face-to-face interactions. For example, I have yet to deliver a conference paper without my (West Yorkshire) accent attracting some comment, a fact that says much about my social and political agendas and those of the commentators, about the context in which they surface, and about the fact I have only been to conferences in England.

Ivor also notes the social and political import of dress and speech in conversation with Barry Troyna, whose own speech and dress explicitly and consciously expressed his allegiance to his background. He goes on to say that what makes people willing to collaborate on research projects is "(o)ften to do with eye contact, body language, chemistry, background, a million things which are quite impossible to legislate or predict" (Sikes, 2011, p. 20). In other words, face-to-face, embodied communication concretely expresses the fact that power is always and already implicit in human relations and interactions. Therefore, in addition to the more prosaic reasons I gave earlier, meeting face to face would to my mind interrupt and add a further dimension to the particular power dynamics inherent in my writing about Ivor Goodson.

Because I was intending to continue using the substance of our discussion subsequent to our meeting, I asked for permission to record it for transcription. I had no firm ideas about how I would use it, although I did consider that I might interweave snippets or segments throughout the book to animate or illustrate the points I was making. However, even as I transcribed it, I became convinced that removing small segments in this way would not only do violence to the whole but would also result in dry and ultimately meaningless extracts, and this was confirmed by my attempts to do so. Concomitant with these activities I was also engaged in thinking through my understanding of "Teaching Ivor Goodson." My conclusion that the transcribed conversation encapsulated all that I considered vital to include in this section might therefore be considered serendipitous—or opportunistic. However, there are other reasons behind my final decision to base this section on the representation of our dialogic encounter.

First and as the opening quotation makes clear, it reflects a mode of scholarship and of representation that Ivor himself favors. He refers, for example, to the way in which interviews lend a "more realistic personal flesh and personal aspiration" to the notion of life politics (2011, p. ix) and indeed I would add that it does this in a more general sense, for example, by infusing theoretical propositions with auto/biographical insights. He also maintains that it provides "a production location for the mutual exploration of meaning and selfhood" (Goodson & Gill, 2011, p. 42). Most importantly, however, face-to-face interaction is not simply a form of *dialogic* or *narrative* encounter (or exchange or interchange as Ivor sometimes refers to them). They are also *pedagogic* encounters that "invoke a 'third voice' which is the voice of the collaboration between the people involved in the narrative encounter" (Goodson & Gill, p. xi).

Talking face to face therefore offered the possibility of congruence between process and product, form and content, and style and substance, which in turn mirrors the internal coherence of Ivor's scholarly endeavors and the linkages between his personal and academic life (I use the term *life/work* to reflect and convey precisely this congruence). Moreover, in some academic cultures the "interview" format is favored above others. As a traveling organic intellectual, Ivor's scholarly contribution has sometimes been made in this way rather than delivered as a lecture or keynote speech, for example, and his book *Life Politics* (2011) also takes this form.

At the risk of sounding deterministic, the high regard Ivor has for face-to-face conversations is to my mind understandable. It is the legacy of being born into an oral culture, although the emphasis on *oral* here can overshadow the importance of the *aural* aspects of this culture, where listening to stories is at least as important as telling them. Ivor acknowledges the contribution that listening to other people makes in the development of his ideas, something that must be understood as having an ethical cadence.

The ethical import of embodied interaction is made more explicit when Ivor informs Jerry Brunetti that "if you make an interpretation, it has to be grounded in data that has been generated face to face with others" (Goodson, 2011, p. 85). He goes on to state that:

> the only way we can ever go across hierarchies is in a face-to-face relationship where you build up a trusting relationship which actually says, in very simple terms, I think I value you as much as you value me. Human beings are pretty sensitive to that. (Goodson, 2011, p. 127)

However, and without downplaying the significance of any of these reasons, I would venture to say that at its heart Ivor wants to meet and talk to people because it is a *social* activity. He emphasizes to Jess Moriarty (2012), for example, that "I am a highly social person" and that his "idea of a good life is a great conversation."

There are, fortuitously, a number of challenges inherent in the broad concept of "Teaching Ivor Goodson" that can be met through using a conversational form of representation. I have already stated that the conceptual lens through which we have read Ivor Goodson was my own creation and that ultimately, it is my reading of him that came into play. Affording some space for his own words goes some way to redressing the balance, although this should not be taken for an attempt to include Ivor's "voice," not least because if Ivor himself had been keen for his "voice" to come through I have no doubt he would have offered an unequivocal commentary to my drafts. But at the same time I would argue that excluding it would also have involved quite some effort on my part. Inasmuch as my purpose here is to create a potential dynamic between the two sections of the book, we can think in terms of the creation of a "third voice," one that transcends the parameters of any individual interpretation.

Another challenge to address in this section is the repositioning of the conceptual lens constituted in the previous section, so that it focuses to a greater extent on matters pertaining to methodology. However, my intention is also to retain a sense of the integration and interplay of methodology with other aspects of his scholarship, and not least with Ivor Goodson the man, rather than to reinforce their distinctiveness. Who Ivor is, what he has done, and the way he has gone about doing it are not only in tandem but in harmony here. Indeed, the main reason I have designated "Reading" and "Teaching" as "sections" of the book rather than "parts" is because, to my mind at least, the former retains a stronger sense of situation in, rather than removal from, a whole.

It is a defining feature of Ivor Goodson's scholarship that his methodologies are grounded in his conviction that theory and practice have to speak to each other if they are to serve the ambitions of criticality and transcendence rather than reinforcing the status quo. The importance of both his conceptual and empirical work therefore does not reside primarily in its "real world" relevance per se, although we have seen that he has an acute sensitivity to material and lived realities. That notwithstanding, on Ivor's terms relevance should be measured by its transformative potential, and methodologies by the extent to which they support him in realizing the aspirations of his soci(ologic)al imagination and the moral obligations of his public intellectual work. It was therefore imperative that, whatever the approach taken in the (re)presentation of this aspect of Ivor Goodson, the move from "Reading" to "Teaching" had to be more in the way of a transition than a rupture.

At the same time it was crucial not to slip from pedagogy into didacticism by representing "Teaching Ivor Goodson" as "How to Teach Ivor Goodson." This would be totally at odds with the notion of pedagogy that Ivor has embraced from the earliest days of his teaching (Goodson, 2005a). I also had to be careful not to create divisions that might undermine my argument for consistency, not only in Ivor's enduring concerns but also in his character and the way he conducts himself. He states unequivocally that "my professional dream is inseparable to my personal dream" (Goodson, 2011, p. 13) and this is indeed the case. It would be a pointless exercise to try and compartmentalize his activities or to try and identify the different "selves" that would make up the whole.

The (moral) significance of this point is apparent when Ivor responds to Irene Turinho, who picks him up on the apparent contradiction between his own conceptualization of himself as a coherent self, with postmodern understandings of the non-unitary self (Goodson, 2011, p. 48). In his answer it is clear that Ivor does not deny the existence of the postmodern fragmented and troubled self. Indeed he sees these selves as "irrefutable facts" (Goodson, 2011, p. 48). But, he explains:

> the only way to remain optimistic in the world is to reassert not the primacy of a singular self, but the primacy of a self which keeps a meaningful narrative going. I see identity as keeping *a meaningful narrative going*. (Goodson, 2011, p. 48, emphasis added)

If one accepts that optimism reflects a particular moral stance and a particular life politics, then it is instructive to hear how Ivor himself goes about keeping his own meaningful narrative going.

A further challenge inherent in the notion of "Teaching Ivor Goodson" relates to the sheer volume of Ivor's work. I have alluded to this several times already, but the following, abridged, email exchange that took place between Liz Briggs, Ivor's PA, and myself not long into my research for this volume captures my trepidation:

Yvonne: The weather is lovely here and my husband has just texted me to say he's gone on a bike ride. Now I feel chained to my desk. Hope it's nice down there.

Liz: Good luck with your work but make sure you stretch your legs!!! I've been chained to the desk getting Ivor's latest book shipshape but at the end now I hope! Good luck with it all.

Yvonne: Tell Ivor he must stop writing. There is so much there already!

Liz: Impossible—have told him and he just goes on . . .

Such a body of work is a repository for a huge range of ideas and concerns, particularly as Ivor has written transnationally and cross-culturally and in the context of the political and social transformations of five decades. How could I ensure that the albeit necessary liberties taken (abridging, summarizing, synthesizing, and so on) did not result in a soulless, prosaic rendition of a profound and captivating original? Inclusion of Ivor's words, recorded, transcribed, and reproduced in written form as they may be, nevertheless offer the best chance of retaining some of the Ivor-ness of the original utterance.

In addition to meeting challenges, there are a number of more positive reasons for presenting this section in dialogic form: it provides a vehicle for accessing the thought processes involved in getting to grips with "big issues"; it animates those aspects of Ivor's character that are located in arenas other than those of his scholarly pursuits; it offers a fresh perspective on his historian's dedication to documents of the past and his historian's insistence on accounting for broader historical conditions in the analysis of contemporary sociological issues; it acts as a conduit to understanding his abhorrence of research methods that are employed for merely "technical" reasons, and which he considers to be impoverished as a result. Finally, it allows me to include reference to issues that do not appear in the previous section and to augment, expand, and develop ideas from a different perspective.

Although I have taken pains to limit my interference throughout the processes of recording, transcription, and analysis, the encounter I had with Ivor has undergone a number of procedures before being depicted here. The most significant of these is my division of a two-part conversation (Ivor went out part way through to fetch sandwiches) into three chapters, each with its own thematic heading. Although arriving here was a protracted process involving many false starts, settling on these areas—biography, scholarship, and learning and pedagogy—seemed an obvious choice in the end, not because it captures some notion of "the essential Ivor Goodson" but because, taken together, they cover the ground over which Ivor himself has consistently ranged over the course of his career. They also provide three different but ultimately convergent departure points from which to take up his contributions: as a man loyal to his beginnings, as a scholar and public intellectual, and as a teacher committed to a socially inclusive agenda.

I have already stated that it is impossible to separate Ivor the scholar from Ivor the man and therefore to exclude an auto/biographical element from the whole would be a serious omission. I have titled the first chapter "Biography" to indicate that we are focusing on a particular approach rather than on Ivor's life story alone. Under the heading of "Scholarship" I have included that which relates to his ideas about approaches to theory-building and research and their relationship with practice. This includes paying attention to the extent to which his career has pushed against both conceptual and empirical boundaries. "Learning and Pedagogy" not only encapsulates but also instantiates his ideas about both. In other words, the material for this chapter was chosen precisely because it demonstrates how the creation of a third voice can be set to the task of furthering knowledge, meaning, and understanding.

In addition to and as a result of this restructuring, I have also re-sequenced parts of the conversation. Because I took pains to limit my involvement here, Ivor's utterances are not re-presented entirely in the order they were made. We are out of synch with the actual conversation as it was recorded and transcribed and therefore Ivor will sometimes refer to something that was said that does not appear in the conversation as it is relayed in the chapter. I have chosen not to disguise this. It does not undermine comprehension and the fact that it serves as a reminder that we are dealing with a crafted account here is to my mind all to the good.

Other than these intrusions, I have done some minimal editing to comply with the exigencies of turning the spoken word into text and have omitted some of what was transcribed if it repeats a point that was made elsewhere. We are not talking about major revisions, however. Ivor can speak at length and develop a complex argument without repeating himself or stumbling over his words. He has the ability to be "on message" and to speak with passion and eloquence for an extended period of time. I have therefore consciously tried to stay as close as possible to Ivor's utterances without also divesting the whole of reminders that we are dealing with a textual representation. For example, for ease of comprehension I have inserted punctuation and I have included notes on references that may be unfamiliar to some readers.

That said, much is lost when turning speech into text. Readers cannot hear the sound of Ivor's hand drumming the table as he emphasizes his points, for example, nor will they catch him smiling mischievously or have much sense of the measured but obviously passionate mode of his delivery. However, the purpose of these chapters is not to provide material for analysis. It is to instantiate and epitomize a particular interactive pedagogy that sits at the heart of Ivor's hopes for an inclusive education system. In this sense we might take the following chapters as a performative representation of what is meant by *Teaching Ivor Goodson.*

Chapter 10

Biography

The conversation I had with Ivor did not begin here but as he consistently argues that the starting point for understanding, for theory, and indeed for teaching and learning is the individual's life story, it would have made little sense to have started elsewhere. In the previous section I emphasized that Ivor does not position the life story as "The Truth." It is instead a departure point for a collaboration whose aim is the creation of knowledge that challenges the status quo, the hegemonic, and the monolithic. Therefore, I am not suggesting that we will get to "know" Ivor Goodson in what follows. This is not a "scoop." But it does provide an insight into and makes some sense of the "meaningful narrative" (Goodson, 2011, p. 48) Ivor employs in his own identity project. In concentrating more on the personal motivations and the "back story" to some of his scholarly foci we have the chance for a richer, more layered understanding of the significance of coherence, consistency, and integrity, not only *within* his scholarship but *between* his scholarly endeavors and other aspects of his life. This chapter epitomizes what is meant by "life/work."

A personal account, then, provides a different vantage point from which to view his theoretical, substantive, and methodological approaches and offers a glimpse into the "inner workings" of his processes. It also animates and substantiates the concepts that constitute the conceptual lens that I fashioned for "Reading Ivor Goodson." In this respect we also have a shift along the continuum from a general reading to the provision of depth and detail. In the previous section I have mentioned several times his tremendous attachment to family, for example, and here we have reference not only to his wife and his son but also to his grandparents and to "ancestral voices" more generally; the discussion of the origins of his interest in history also modulates his insistence on the inclusion of historical awareness in sociological analysis and theory building. We join Ivor in the narration of his personal imperatives but I am reiterating that the import of this mode of presentation does not rest on a notion that inclusion of a person's words yields a more authoritative voice. Its power is derived instead in the emergence of a "third voice," the synthesis of face-to-face interaction and collaboration and the outcome of the fair trade between two actors.

I start this conversation at what I consider to be a pivotal, if not *the* most pivotal, moment in Ivor's life. I do so for the reasons mentioned earlier and also in response to a request to "put some flesh on Ivor's working-class bones."

Yvonne: Going back to your youth, I wanted to talk about the story of when you worked in the crisp factory and then your teacher came. You tell this story in an almost nonchalant, "Why don't you come back to school?" "Oh alright then I will" way. How big of a deal was that in your life? Was this an epiphanic moment or is that an interpretation I have overlaid on it?

Ivor: I think it's a massive moment. For me it's such an important story because it shows that the trajectory that I was on was pretty much the trajectory of the tribe. It is what happened to all my cousins and all of my mates. They all went to work in factories at 15. That's what we did. That's what we all did. That's what I did. It's all I knew. When I talk of our journey and our polished reflexivity and our border crossings, we're talking about later. We're talking about the fortune of the trajectory that happened. But the reality is like all the people that we're talking about, whether upper class or lower class, I was encased by tribal understandings. I had no social imagination beyond that. I always had a somewhat deviant sense of the school, that it wasn't for me, that it wasn't serving my purposes, and that I was interested in other questions but I never had the sense that I would transcend the social order in any way or that I would be anything other than a manual worker. That was built into the logic of the situation. My dad already had my gas fitter's tools and bag prepared for my apprenticeship and had already set up my apprenticeship for that, so it was either factories or it was being a gas fitter like dad and dad being a gas fitter was a massive step forward from the tribes of Goodson who had always been landless labourers going right back to 1712. So he'd already made the breakthrough to be a gas fitter.

So I think it's really difficult to revisit the 15-year-old self but I know the 15-year-old self was most interested in the things we've talked about today. It was most interested in nights out, in getting a motorbike, a Tiger Trophy, in having girlfriends, in buying clothes, Teddy Boy clothes. That was the 15-year-old Ivor's preoccupation. He wasn't terribly interested in learning and when he took his nine "O" levels he did only get one. It wasn't where his head was at all. So was it a major intervention by another? Yes. This was somebody coming in with the kind of reflexivity we've been talking about intervening in my life and saying, "Look you silly young sod. You've got something here. You're an impossible kid but you're quite bright. Why don't you come back and I'll steer you through. I'll share my cognitive map of the world with you. I'll draw you a map. I'll tell you what a university is. I'll draw you a map for the interview and I'll teach you economics and history." That's what he did. And of course it changed my life.

I don't know if you've been watching a programme on the grammar schools[1] because that's what this was, a grammar school. It's absolutely fascinating. They interview about 20 people, well-known politicians and the like, and every one of them when they talk about this moment bursts into tears. It's an emotional rupture this moment, because what was happening in that moment—now I know but then I didn't, I knew nothing then—was that the whole trajectory and the whole socially embedded nature of my position in the world was being challenged by the reflexivity and strategic sophistication of somebody else. Not me I hasten to add. My intuitions were not in any way primary or superior at this time at all. It was somebody shattering the socially embedded nature of my tribal position and that was what was so crucial about it. There is a debate here to be had about whether, for the small group who went there, the grammar school was a good mechanism for doing that and I think there is an argument that it was and that in some ways for that small group it might have been a better dis-embedding process than comprehensives were. I've always thought that and I wrote about that when I trained as a teacher and I got a C- from Bernstein for doing it because . . .

Yvonne: It didn't fit.

Ivor: It didn't fit with the leftist thing. But there is an argument about that, which one would have to revisit and you'd have to revisit in the light of current reforms and so on. That's the nuance coming in. That's the complexity of blind tribal faith in comprehensives when actually there are issues there and there are issues that need to be discussed.

So to go back to the 15-year-old self—didn't know much about the world. My gaze was not on this at all. My gaze was on having a bloody good time and I do remember when I got into the sixth form reading an article by somebody called Lord Chandos, who I'd never heard of, and he said something that was absolutely astonishing to me and it blew me away. He said the best years of his life were his 20s and 30s when he was building a career. And for me that was absolutely exceptional because the world I was in knew that 15, 16, or 17 were the best years and after that there was nothing but labour. I knew that, and something in me must have known that this was a trajectory that you maybe want to get out of by the end of your teens. I knew instinctively things like that. That I was at the high point of working class life, which is you're 15 you've got a bit of money in your pocket, most of your mates are at work, you can go off doing whatever you like, you have a motorbike, you're free. But then what's beginning is a lifetime of slavery.

And he caught me just at that moment where I could see everybody in my cohort getting these rubbish jobs like I got and I could see them coming home tired and I could see that the money in their pockets and the motorbikes were paid for by a high price of labour.

Because I was a September-born kid I was a year ahead. Even though I was 15 all of my mates were 16, so I had a year's grace and I could go back to school without losing a year in a sense, at a time where the price, the downside of raffish working-class life, began to become clearer and clearer and clearer. Kids were tired at work and snappy and I could see the peak was over. And I'd wanted the peak. I always wanted it both ways. I wanted the peak but by the time I returned to school, on a provisional one year basis to try and get some "O" levels, I'd become really interested in school. This guy was teaching me a subject I adored—economic history—and I have to admit my gaze finally began to settle on knowledge. And being typically obsessive, once I got interested, god I was interested. I mean the years in the sixth form, it's like *The History Boys*.[2] We were a small group and I can remember the names of all of them. It was a male grammar school of course. Yeah I was absolutely captivated by doing history and economics and geography. My gaze was totally on it. The street began to recede. I still had my weekends out with all the kids who had gone to secondary mods[3] and who were now in factories. I never left to go to university. I always stayed in my village and they remained my friends right through university.

So I never really went away but intellectually my appetite had been whetted and once whetted that was the beginning of intellectual curiosity of a major sort. So to answer your question. It was epiphanic not because of anything to do with my own reflexivity although there might have been some intuitive senses here. Pasteur says chance favours the prepared mind and I believe that and having experienced the crisp factory I'd done that now. It wasn't just the idea of money in my pocket. I'd lived a tedious job on a conveyor belt. I often think of myself now, and what you had was a conveyor belt coming along with crisp packets on and I stood between two older ladies and as the crisp packet came on you picked it up, shook it and put it down so the top could be sealed. That was my job from eight o'clock in the morning till six o'clock at night six days a week, so when I went to bed I was still doing that with my hands at night.

Yvonne: It breaks my heart to think of that.

Ivor: That was the future and my mate was there till he was 65. So that's what happened and so to answer your question, I think therefore I had seen some of that. I knew what I was in for. I knew what my mates were in for and it had lost its gloss. OK there was money in your pocket but I knew the price now. So he timed it beautifully because he'd always wanted me to stay on and I just told him to sod off. I was a difficult kid, a real rough diamond I would say. You can imagine. I often look back on myself and you've got this one Teddy Boy, always in trouble and wouldn't study. I just wouldn't. I talked to him afterwards, because I thanked him several times, and he said, "I just knew that you were bright in spite of everything. You worked very hard to conceal it from everybody but it just came out in certain questions. You just had it." Now that's something you can't wish away in this analysis of the world is it? So I don't know. It was a key moment and it was largely the intervention of somebody else and pretty serendipitous let's face it. There were two or three socialist teachers in the school, two sixth form teachers, and there was a concern for the few kids from the working class. They definitely had a programme, a socialist programme, to try and help out.

Yvonne: So not entirely serendipitous?

Ivor: No. But it's his strategy not mine. That's the point I'm making. If you're looking at a sort of model of social change, it's his intervention. I think it was beginning to be fertile soil. He'd badgered me in the fifth form and I remember telling him, "No way. I'm off. There's better things than this. You get on with what you're doing but I've got better fish to fry." I remember saying all that to him. Six months on . . .

Yvonne: You've fried those fish.

Ivor: Isn't it funny to think of him saying, "I'll go over." It's quite a journey to the crisp factory. It's an admirable piece of intervention when you look back now. I've got a lot to thank him for.

Yvonne: This comes back to the art and craft of immersing yourself in someone's life. I think knowing when to intervene, the nature of that intervention, how far to go, is not easy. There's a line between that and interference and voyeurism, social engineering . . .

Ivor: I suppose that's what we're looking for all the while you and I. I refer to it as pedagogic moments. My job is the endless pursuit of pedagogic moments and I suppose it comes from being on the receiving end of a quintessential pedagogic moment where somebody times their intervention so beautifully that your whole trajectory is changed. I mean how clever was that of this person? If I could do that once or twice I'd be pleased. So I think my life since then has been a constant attempt to replicate that moment for others. And that would only seem fair if I could. I can think of a few times I've done that but it's difficult.

Yvonne: You mentioned loving history. I think you're a historian to your bones. Is that due to the influence of your teacher?

Ivor: I've always been like that. It precedes the influence of my teacher although that inscribed history as the way forward, but I remember one of the epiphanic moments in my life was before I learned to read, although I didn't learn to read till I was 8. I was walking in the fields with my spaniel and at the back of the council estate were a lot of open fields still, and high on the hill was a place called Bulmershe Court which became Bulmershe College of Education which became the School of Education at Reading University. It was an old Georgian house where Henry Addington had been prime minister and it was the Whebles[4] who had colonised the whole area and had expelled my family from their cottage. I still remember vividly looking up at that house and having this overwhelming sense of history, the history of my village, my tribe, that house and thinking, "I'd love to find out more about history." And this is a 7 year-old child who can't read but obviously is having thoughts about the social order. Historical thoughts. I always ask "When?" "When did you do that?" "How long were you in teaching?" It's always historical questions. That's just my angle of approach and maybe it's my way of establishing continuity over time. We've talked about how do you keep that continuing sense of self over time in the face of multiple settings and environments. Probably that's the way.

Yvonne: I have also noticed that the way you go about things is never an entire rejection or ever an entire embrace.

Ivor: I think one of the difficulties which I get from attempts to translate my work into other languages, is that my work is nuanced. It is never black and white and there are two things you note about me that are correct. I never want to define my own orthodoxy, my own brand name by which I will be known and I never want disciples. I think it's to do with the nuanced understandings of the world which I think historians particularly have. I'm interested in the messy middle ground of social contestation. It's not simple to say capitalism's good or bad. Sometimes it's better than at other times. Nothing is simple. Marx is sometimes right sometimes wrong. I am never drawn to these grand narratives. I was talking about this with my son the other day—he was sitting right where you are now. One of the key events in my life was fortuitous. When I was at the London School of Economics I was invited to go in a small group to the Soviet Union. I travelled with Cosmos travel. It was one of the first times they really opened up to small groups to travel across the Soviet Union and given my class background you might think I'd be drawn to Communism and I was certainly very interested in exploring Soviet Russia. But going there and seeing the intractability of the Soviet system and its failure to deliver and its colonisation by the elites early on, I was only 23 at the time, helped me from having any kind of massive, grand, utopian beliefs. I do have utopian beliefs. I have my own New Jerusalem and I know what it looks like and it looks broadly social democratic and it looks not unlike Attlee's government of 1945. It's embodied. But I never went for the grand utopian schemes and I think I was incredibly fortunate to be able to go to Russia at that time because I think I instinctively might have been drawn to some rather un-nuanced thing. So from that moment on my understandings of the great Cold War battles were always fairly nuanced. I knew if my tribe was to survive in these situations it would be a nuanced survival, it would be a contested survival, it would be a difficult survival and there weren't any simple places to fight. There never were.

Yvonne: I think this points to the way you seem able to make your prefigurative and strategic politics work in tandem, which is a difficult thing to do in the academy. To put it another way, you hold your line. How do you manage to do that?

Ivor: You had to fight in this difficult way that you describe. Yes. It's been really hard to stand in the same place over a long period. I make no bones about that. I think you take a lot of hits for that, especially in the academy, but you pick yourself up and go on. I can't complain. I've had a marvellous career. You could say "You're a hypocrite. You've had a marvellous career. What are you talking about?" What I'm talking about, to go back to the work, is that it's not easy to read because it's nuanced, it's interested in complexity and I think I've always stayed in the same place. There is nothing I've ever written that I'd be ashamed for my dad to read or my mum to read. They would read it and they would know.

Yvonne: It's interesting you mention your parents here. I was talking with my son the other day and he told me that in having my dad's name he feels he has something to live up to. I don't want him to feel he can't be his own person and make mistakes and all of that, but on the other hand I was heartened to think that something was being continued, especially of course if you think that something was good, which clearly I do.

Ivor: That's important because that's continuity beyond self isn't it? And I think that's the spin off from standing in the same place. If you gave yourself in to ego projects like orthodoxies and disciples, what you are doing is cutting yourself off from the authentic continuation of yourself I think. So I think you have to move beyond narcissistic projects of selfhood if you are to ever have new generations take up your theme. If you're just the great grand hero of your story, like the master builder in Ibsen, you're strapped to the mast of your own ego. That's why I've never wanted orthodoxies or disciples but I certainly have wanted to lock into the continuity of struggle of past generations of my family. One of the best things my son ever said to me was, "Dad I understand your project. In many ways I share it." That's the most exciting thing he could have ever said to me. Of course he'll play it out differently in his own way but he understands what that is about. And you'll see in the latest book—it's about my grandparents. It's dedicated to them— I'm trying to reach back into those ancestral voices. Strangely enough the chapter I'm writing at the moment is on ancestral voices. It's about what gets transmuted and passed on to you in some unspoken ways from a family which never read and wrote. How do you pick up where they are on things?

What kind of stories get passed on? So in a sense your make up is part of that trajectory because I haven't invented this place from which I stand. It was there and it is part of our family trajectory and long may it be so. I'm just part of that chain of transmission. And if I went for this big ego project I wouldn't be, I'd be standing aside from that tradition. We come and we go. All things must pass but I think if you try and create an orthodoxy you're trying to fight against that. You're almost trying to fight against your own mortal self. I don't see any point in fighting against that because of course we all die. What you have to have done while you were here is stand in the right place. Sounds a bit pious doesn't it?

Yvonne: Well that's the problem, isn't it? It can sound pious and I think the reason it does is that there is a real moral element to the idea of holding the line and I think the moment that comes into play, it almost becomes a dirty word because it becomes associated with moralizing and trying to foist your moral position on somebody else.

Ivor: I think there are a number of problems. It looks like moral high ground that you are trying to claim, it looks like you are trying to claim this incredible working-class hero mantle. There are all sorts of problems with it aren't there? But I would say that one tries to argue against such a position. In other words the forces of domination are well-practiced in finding ways to denigrate this position. "He's a man with a chip on his shoulder. He's a working-class hero. He a morally pious burke." All of these are ways of saying, "OK maybe he is standing in the right place but we don't want him to stand there. It's not a good place for the dominant groups to have people like him there. So let's have a whole set of stigmata." You said earlier it must have been difficult. What is difficult is that there are available a whole range of stigmata for someone trying to act against domination. Of course there are. There are a whole range of other academic stigmata. "He's never here. He's always on the road." Or "He just did it for his own material success. He's clearly successful, he's made some money." All true. So there's a vast range of domination penetrated stigmata to be dealt with but that's not a reason not to proceed, is it?

Yvonne: No. But for example wherever I've worked I've always acquired the label "bolshie." Even when I've tried to be really nice. All you have to do is ask one awkward question and that's it.

Ivor: But that's the stigmata available to the cross-questioning intellectual. But it's what we came to do, isn't it?

Yvonne: I guess. Yes. I come from a bolshie family, an interfering family that if they see things going on they never walk by on the other side.

Ivor: Well we shouldn't walk by on the other side should we? There is an absolute continuity between us there.

Yvonne: This makes it sound very noble but actually it is just as much a case of not being able to keep my trap shut, to hold my tongue.

Ivor: So a lack of control. That would seem to be our history.

Yvonne: Yes, a complete lack of self-control.

Ivor: Anyone looking at us would say they have been completely under-socialised those two, we've done a bad job on both of them. They've not been disciplined properly. In that sense society has failed with us two. We've looked at it, we've questioned it, we've gazed at it. We've not done any of the things we should have done.

Yvonne: No, I've rarely done any of the things I should have done.

Ivor: You have said it's been hard and in some ways it has.

Yvonne: Well it has, but it's like when my friend asked out of the blue if there is anything I would change and I honestly could not think of one thing. I'm pretty much alright where I am. I don't need to change anything.

Ivor Me too. It's what we are. It's the way I'm made. In some ways there are no choices. We've been talking about all these contextual choices, but in some ways there are no choices.

Yvonne: Well, I try to hold my line but I readily admit not always. Sometimes I've said, "Oh no this is too hard" and I've played along but in the end it always gets you because that is a false way of living no matter how hard holding the line is. But it is hard on a daily basis, which makes it sound as if you are this great crusader, which I don't feel at all. I feel very cowardly.

Ivor: That is why being seen as morally pious is so hard to take because you know you're just a malleable human being who's failed as many times as they've succeeded. That's what we are. Of course we are. So it isn't about heroism. It's more likely to be about cowardice. I can think of many cowardly things I've done.

As you just said—I'm not putting words in your mouth—we find our position and we move in and out of engagement. That's exactly what we do, whether it's in relationships or whatever it is. And of course in that sense you're autonomous, in that sense you're a free agent, in that sense you're an autodidact—all of those things we are, I am. So we started by saying how hard it's been and yes there's been aspects of the social work that have been difficult but given what I've just said it's been a great game to play because in that sense there is a privilege to that kind of gaze that we've been given, isn't there?

Yvonne: There absolutely is.

Ivor: You can turn every misfortune into fortune and in some ways being born poor is a misfortune. In other ways, if you're lucky, it's enormously fortunate to have all of those things, so the alchemy of the situation is to turn misfortune into fortune, to turn marginality into commonsensical observation.

Yvonne: Well that's the thing, isn't it? It's about being on the margins but also knowing how to step in and out of it so that you feel it, you have that experience of it and then you can retreat to the margins again.

Ivor: That marginality does give you a different gaze because in a sense you are looking through the bars, you're looking through the windows. I feel that's how I am with society. And as you rightly say one moves in and out— of engagement, of other things. So maybe it's not just about commonsensicality. It's about marginality because if you're fully involved in the game in a paradoxical way you don't understand what the game's about.

Yvonne: I used to think everyone thought in that marginal way.

Ivor: They don't. They're too immersed in their script. A good example would be David Cameron who's born in the middle of a game, born into privilege but who has no idea how to play the game. So it's actually rather interesting if you've got all that insider kind of stuff, actually you are caught inside the maze. You don't understand the maze and perhaps the great privilege of marginality is that we're allowed to understand it in different ways. And what that does is rework privilege. It's like that story of when Ted Hughes meets Sylvia Plath's mother, I was just writing it today. You'll love this story. So Sylvia Plath takes Ted Hughes to meet her mother in this wonderful, affluent New England house. He's baffled by the richness of it because he comes from a very proletarian background. As they are leaving she tells Ted Hughes that Sylvia has had it very hard and Ted Hughes says, "Oh, why's that?" And Sylvia's mother says it's because she has not had the privilege Ted has had of having had to fight for everything and of knowing why she does things.

Yvonne: That does reconfigure privilege.

Ivor: Well that's why I have a nuanced view I think and why I would be strangely sympathetic to some of the sad characters currently in government. I think they are just caught in this awful womb of privilege and people out in the world know they don't understand. They know they don't have a clue. They know they make all these mistakes about pasties and things people eat every day, and in a way it's a sadness of privilege as defined. I think the real privilege in a funny way is to be marginal and to find your own way. It's back to Ted Hughes. You find your own voice, on your own terms, on the margins and you move in and out of engagement. That has to be a lovely position. Let's not knock it.

Yvonne: It also makes it difficult to get the Ivor-ness onto the page.

Ivor: Personally—and don't think I've thought about it strategically at all—but just personally the way I have kept my academic passion going—or social passion, I don't see myself as an academic—is in moving between different genres and different settings. I think I've constantly wanted in a way to keep on the move. And I think that is what I've always done in life. Physically and socially and in every other way. I've made a game of those border crossing at both those levels because I think when you're border crossing you're on social alert, watching. And that's the moment I love. And so I like to move between genres and orthodoxies. I would hate to be the kind of person who wrote this book and created this orthodoxy and spent the rest of his life talking about it with his disciples around him. That to me would be absolutely a nightmare. How boring would that be? And yet I recognise that is what a lot of people want.

Yvonne: Oh you've mentioned a word there! I also have a great abhorrence for boredom. I think it signals that you have lost some inquisitiveness about life, some of that curiosity. In some ways it's no bad thing to be in a place of acceptance and contentment. But to lose that critical edge and curiosity and inquisitiveness somehow implies you have reached a place of wisdom and perhaps that is overrated. I guess this is really a question about getting older.

Ivor: Well obviously I am getting older and yesterday my son was sitting there where you are now and he said to me, "Do you feel older, Dad?" And I said, "Yeah, I do. I am starting to travel less." And he said "Well you don't seem older" and I suppose he was also saying, "You don't seem wiser either." Clearly, chronologically, I am getting older. But in some ways I don't feel old because the work I am doing now is in some ways more interesting to me than anything I've ever done. That is what is so fascinating. It would be very difficult to stop. However, there are certain things that do change. One concession I am making to age is less travel. One of the things I have always believed in is that you should remain on the road physically as well as mentally. That you should be a global organic intellectual seeing what's going on. That's beginning to stop. I'm beginning to have less of a compulsion to travel all the time. I've basically been on the road for 40 years. Sometimes nine months of the year I'd be traveling, even recently maybe three months. I'm just beginning to feel I don't need to do that to get these border crossing moments. Now maybe that's more to do with inner peace or fatigue I don't know. But I definitely don't have quite that imperious sense of the hero going round the world. I don't want that any more. So I'm settling to some degree but I'm not settling in terms of genre crossing or in terms of new intellectual agendas. I don't see that ever receding I'm afraid. It's the way I am in the world I think. I'm just a curious little boy really.

Yvonne: I would hate to think I could ever just accept things.

Ivor: That would be death for me. That would be a very morbid condition, to have to accept anything as immutable and certainly the social order which I regard with great concern and contempt. I shan't ever buy into the social order. I shall never want to be part of any establishment. I'm not interested in it and it represents many of the things I don't want in the world. So I shan't join that. I shan't get fixed in that sense. I think we shall always be curious don't you think, Yvonne?

Yvonne: Well I don't want to be essentialist in any way but I ask myself if I was born curious or if it was something created in me.

Ivor: I've just had a letter from Ragna [Adlandsvik]—it was a letter to me and Mary—and she says at the bottom, "Ivor, you'll always be a happy and curious boy." In some ways it's not fun to occupy the position we do and to lose as often as we do and the mystery to me is that somehow I've always found it a happy experience. Obviously it's optimism of the will and my will is optimistic and even given the state of late capitalism I'm still relatively optimistic as a human being.

Yvonne: Optimism can be seen as a moral stance.

Ivor: It's a duty in a way but I do feel it. I take things lightly at one level. My son again said, "You're so serious about all this social justice stuff, aren't you?" I said, "Yes I am but I also take life lightly." It's a light business. I am passionate about my purposes but they don't weigh me down. Maybe that's just temperament. I don't think it has anything to do with capacities or skill or genius. My mum said I was always a happy child. Mindlessly so I think. I didn't read till I was 8. I wasn't interested. I was just happy.

Yvonne: I don't think I'm quite that happy or have quite that lightness but I never take things more seriously than I can bear.

Ivor: That's the point. I'm sure we do take things heavy at times and we are both serious about our purposes. I have no doubt about that. But it's how you carry it and how you develop a social milieu as well. There are a lot of questions about how a long academic life of contestation is lived. And one of the questions is what sort of social milieu do you create? Most of my friends tend to be certainly outside the academy but also outside of the establishment. And that's always been so. I have always had a hinterland, a quite easy hinterland. It's always been pubs and clubs and football, all locker rooms in some ways, but it's always been all of those things. I've always had a pleasant hinterland.

Yvonne: Me too. And a lot of that for me is my family. I come from a big family and we were lucky to have grown up in the neighbourhood we did. It's only now we are going to funerals as our old neighbors pass on that we realize how lucky we were.

Ivor: I am very proud of the people I came from. Very proud.

Chapter 11

Scholarship

The primary substantive foci of the conversation that follows are the activities that, to a large extent, describe the parameters of an academic career: research, theoretical and conceptual development, writing and the contribution to knowledge. All of these can be accessed through Ivor's writings but approaching these topics through the medium of a dialogic exchange has the potential to generate insights into the processes and ideas that underpin and inform his thinking and his position. We also get a richer and more evocative portrayal of some of the key aspects of Ivor's academic identity (which he would rather depict as a social identity), in which the centrality of holding on to social values and the interplay between prefigurative and strategic politics are particularly significant.

With regards to our discussion about the research aspects of scholarship, we are also able to cover some ground here that was not part of our purview in "Reading Ivor Goodson." Most importantly, Ivor gives his views on the ethics of research and on methodologies for researching with human beings, which also inform his ideas about the politics and relationships of power in research situations. In setting out his thoughts about what we might usefully call "researcher identity," including the qualities, conduct, and duties that attach to the role, we can detect both normative and practical aspects. His insistence that as a researcher one needs to stay alert to changes on the broader stage and to be prepared to move in and out of different sites of contestation and engagement, for example, makes sense in the increasingly competitive battle for funded research. However, it is apparent that this way of working has served, first and foremost, the demands of a public intellectual role. It has been for Ivor an enactment of his life politics and the strategic application of his prefigurative politics.

Ivor's words articulate two significant approaches to the theory-building aspects of his academic labor. First, by invoking the notion of "the tides of time" as they apply to current events and real world situations, Ivor animates his conviction that taking a historical perspective leads to theoretical understandings. We are thereby provided with an insight into the alchemy of turning learning from actual events and happenings into theories whose reach extends beyond the parameters of their origins. Second, by making simple statements and then layering those with complexities Ivor demonstrates the gradational, incremental processes that contribute to his theoretical work.

I start the conversation, however, with a discussion of where research and theory should now be located and question whether, as academics, we have perhaps been less than nimble in keeping up with the ever-changing locus of power.

Yvonne: I've been thinking a great deal about whether it's institutional sites that we should really be focusing on or is it personal subjective sites? Like you, I have always believed that personal sites and subjectivity is where we need to start the unravelling process but the Hillsborough inquiry[1] and the role of the BBC in the Jimmy Savile affair[2] made me wonder whether we have taken our eye off the ball and that maybe we should be focusing on institutional sites after all.

Ivor: I think that's a good point. It links with the most interesting point that you raise in life politics. Is it an over-estimate to say that there's a disjuncture between all of the institutional and curriculum work and the life politics work and I'm convinced you're right, that actually what we have is a continuity here and a moving between sites of resistance and of course those sites come into play, go out of play, come back in play, literally to use the Hillsborough analogy, and yes they are coming back into play, there's no doubt about that, and I think the way that the curriculum debate is being played so ineptly will bring that back into play. One of the things that's bringing so much back into contestation is the unbelievable incompetence of the group of people that have taken over. They just don't have a clue. They're born to rule but they're born to ruin. People are not stupid. They've cottoned on that this is a bunch of dodos.

Yvonne: They are a bunch of dodos.

Ivor: But what that means is that various things you would have thought would have been signed and sealed at certain times in history are not. In a way you can say the same thing about what happened when Yeltsin came to power in Russia. What happened was, he basically promoted the free market and it was assumed therefore that the free market would fill all the gaps and Russia would be marketised. In the event the free market did not fill the gaps, the state came back in and filled the void and you've got a new form of contestation there which is geo-politically quite significant. So I think we've gone through a period of free market triumphalism which has blown us all away from the mid-1990s till about now. Now we're seeing what's bound to be a counter-reaction of some sort. It's an interesting struggle now because basically neo-liberalism does have the levers of power of most institutional sites but that doesn't mean that the contest is over. I think Hillsborough shows that. But it's amazing how long they sat on it. Establishments can do that.

Yvonne: Is the success, if you want to call it that, due to the pressure exerted becoming unbearable, or is it because someone thought "Now's the time to finally get rid of it."

Ivor: I'd be inclined always towards the latter.

Yvonne: Me too.

Ivor: I think it was time to make some concessions in some places because it was so crass everywhere so it was a symbolic piece of action which doesn't have much implication in fact. Most of the people involved are dead, have moved on and so on and I'm not sure it's going to lead to a serious questioning of the way Establishments do things. I'm not sure there will be a serious questioning of what the banks did to people. So yes the contest moves on to a new terrain and there are some victories that we might not have expected. But the overarching narrative still seems to be primarily controlled by neo-liberalism. Once you let the free market genie out of the bottle and once you let it into the health service and into the BBC there aren't many prefigurative spaces or institutions that are unaffected by it. So both yes and no. No, I don't think we took our eye off the ball. But yes, we always need our eye on the ball because there are always chances, there are always contests even at the institutional level. But for me that has to be continuously invigorated by an ongoing life politics. It can't be situated only in the institutional spaces. So to rephrase the question, you are right there is a continuity across all the work that goes back 40 years and it is basically to do with understanding oppression and domination in its various sites, but it's also concerned with where the main sites of interaction and contestation are and those inevitably move and shift over time.

I would still argue that at this point in the cycle of neo-liberal hegemony it is important that people have their life politics as a place to nurture and keep up their moral positions. They can move in and out of the institutional sites from that base. But putting all your money on the institutional, which is what we did in the 1960s, seems to me to be a mistake because subjectivity is so easily structured in those spaces as we are seeing with new generations. So you see the argument I am making. It's the place we keep holy and I think for a while in the 1960s and early 1970s, institutions were the place that you could just put your money on because you could work out all of your politics within them. Then they became increasingly saturated with market ideologies and it was harder to work out your position in those spaces so you had to in a sense regress to life politics to nurture your position, to hold your line, whilst moving in and out of the institutions while you did it. And it may be over time that more spaces, more contests will open up in the institutions and we can move back there but for the moment I would argue that so substantial is the hegemony that life politics and prefigurative politics are the right place to do it.

Yvonne: I agree with you and what seems to happen for me is that I work out my position and then these big things happen and I go back to questioning that.

Ivor: What you are saying is perfectly correct which is that one has to be constantly alert to institutional and other contests and contexts because there are always possibilities. So what we want to avoid is regressing to an individualised life politics. Of course we can't do that. Of course we've got to look at all the collective sites whether they be institutional or extra institutional which I would argue might be a better place to look actually at the moment. You know UK Uncut.[3] There are a whole range of social movements which I would sign up to if I had half a chance. So I mean that's where I'm coming from. You never regress to your individual life politics. That would be just atomistic and fatal and that would be what Bauman[4] is warning against. Never that. But you nurture that as a site for ongoing engagement. That's all I'm saying. The disagreement is only about what are the sites of engagement at any point in time because without engagement there's no point in life politics. I'm saying that they change—you move in and out of different sites and sometimes it's wonderful. You can go into an institutional site which pretty much lives out your dreams. I think mixed ability classrooms, National Health wards where everybody, rich and poor, were together, those were sites where you could literally live out your dreams. Well, they're trying to close most of those sites so it's harder but they can be opened again and they are being opened in certain places so you're on red alert all the time, you polish up your life politics, never let it get individualised and atomised, always use it to move into public engagement if you can.

Yvonne: You state that you are not a multiple self and have talked about how that works in a postmodern atmosphere if you like, where stable, unilateral, progressive narratives of the self with a chronological sequence are being undone. And yet, no matter what area of your work I have looked at, I sense Ivor's presence. I do understand that might work, but how does it? How does the Ivor-ness of it all come through?

Ivor: One line of argument in the postmodern discourses, some which I disagree with, some which I agree with, would say that such continuity, such coherence is in a way to be distrusted. I don't take that view. I take quite the opposite view and you can see in the discussion we've just had how both of us are willing to embrace the multiplicity of engagement possibilities over time. They shift and change over time and in that sense you have multiple selves. But what I'm saying is I take a continuing preoccupation into those multiple engagements. So I don't see a great inconsistency between the argument that you can have a continuing preoccupation and in that sense a continuing self and therefore some continuing coherence of self alongside the multiplicity and the flexibility of response and the re-selfing and everything that I write about. I think if there weren't an Ivor-ness or an Yvonne-ness to it, it would be the most strange postmodern phenomenon. And yes, I also recognise that kind of human being is being bought into existence whose self is performed in different ways for different technological sites and collective sites and who don't seem to have a continual coherent sense of what they are about in the world.

I very much like the work of Salmon[5] who has written about the empty self. He says that what is happening in America is the systematic production of empty selves. Now I think that is a phenomenon that is being bought into existence and it fits beautifully with a consumption-orientated economy. You fill the empty self with consumption. It explains I think a great deal about the form of bodies you see in North America and increasingly in Britain. People are filling up the empty selves with food and consumption. But it argues against moving away from a position where there are coherence-seeking continuities.

So to summarise. Yes it is true there is a multiplicity of different sites for selfhood to play itself out. It is not therefore true that you do not have some essential, abiding, and continuous preoccupations and I don't think it should be so because to paraphrase the old song, "The fundamental things apply as time goes by." They do. Does domination cease under postmodernism? Does oppression cease? Does capitalism cease to do what it's always done? No, of course it jolly well doesn't. You don't need a multiplicity of perspectives to understand some continuities and if you forego your own continuity how are you going to understand the continuities of domination and oppression? It's not a multiplicity game. In some ways it's a continuous act of domination and oppression. If you don't look at that in a continuous and coherent way how would you look at it? So I see no great contradiction between postmodern selfhood having multiple sites of engagement and a continuing sense of coherent purpose.

Yvonne: I don't feel the contradiction, but I did find it difficult to explain.

Ivor: I think it is. I think there was a time when postmodernism swept the field, especially if you were arguing from a coherent masculinised position. As an old white man it was virtually impossible to have a voice of any kind of coherence at all because you were almost devalued in the moment of speaking, quite rightly in some ways because you were representative of old forms of domination just by the way you were embodied. So there was a time when it was very difficult to have a voice, even if it was one against domination because you were positioned as one of the dominators. I don't think that is the case any longer but at its height postmodernism seemed to silence opposition to domination in the moment of its speaking. The moment of tyrannous postmodernism seems to have passed. It did also alert us to the multiplicity of selfhood, it alerted us to diversity, to different orientations. It served a whole range of wonderful political processes, so I don't have a problem with postmodernism, but it did have the capacity to dissolve that notion of central purpose which has to be at the heart of opposing domination. So there was a good side and a bad side. The good side was substantial, the bad side was erosive of critiques of power.

Yvonne: The academy and especially academic language isn't suited to expressions of complexity, nuance, and shifts. It prefers you to take a clear position. Writing about this aspect of your scholarship led me to appreciate more the challenges involved.

Ivor: I think the way that most people write who pursue fame and fortune, shall we say, is that they write now in a very simple bullet point, tight, orthodoxy promoting way. In some ways it's a mystery to me, given the difficulty of some of it, that my work found an audience at all if I'm honest, because even the first books are pretty difficult books and they're very English books. I was genuinely mystified that they went well at all. *School Subjects and Curriculum Change* was a fairly obscure PhD dissertation on England in the 1960s. It's heavily nuanced. It's very complicated. How such a book got out there is still a mystery to me. I didn't set out to do that. I just wanted to understand things myself and wrote it down. Lots of bullet points, boxes, simple ideas, appealing to practitioners, is not the way I write.

Yvonne: But there are certain things in your writing that do strike a chord with people. I think there is an appeal to lived reality. I laughed with sheer relief in some parts of *School Subjects* because yes, that's what it was like. Huge battles over territory and exam success and the best students. It was actually like that.

Ivor: So maybe we are getting at something else here which is, yes it's nuanced and yes it's not in conventional, academic, orthodoxy producing mode but I would like to think it still holds on to a commonsensical look at daily reality because there must be a reason why a book that is not written in an orthodox way, which does not simplify, nonetheless seems to speak about understood reality to many punters. There must be something in there that is a commonsensical gaze on the world.

Yvonne: I think that is absolutely what it is.

Ivor: I think it is that you and I have not been successfully socialised into seeing the world as we are meant to see it. We still see it as outsiders looking in. In that specific sense we see commonsensically what most people have already had partially obscured by the way that domination works. That would be my own slightly self-congratulatory notion of why these books take off. It is that they actually reside in a place of the commonsense gaze. You just look at the world and you say, "Well actually that's not what's going on at all. What's going on is a battle for resources. Come on. Be real. It's not about academic debates about subjects. It's just about money and resources. Come on. You know that and I know that and every teacher who's ever taught knows that so don't give me this other guff. Don't give me these kind of arguments that Gove's[6] talking about, about subject knowledge being holy and pristine. It's not about that at all. It's about social reproduction and resources." So it's holding on to what it's really about and that's slightly different from it being nuanced. It's saying actually reality is messy and complicated but there are certain enduring facts about it and common sense tells you if you're willing to listen, that's it.

Yvonne: I think that's why I found the curriculum chapter so hard to write. I noticed myself going round and round until I finally got to the point, to understanding why you came to these realizations. But that was necessary. I had to get through the whole back story before I understood, yes, this is why Ivor came to these realizations.

Ivor: But in a way everybody knew that. Why didn't they write about it? That's what always baffles me. It's only common sense.

Yvonne: There was something in the book you wrote with Scherto Gill about "deconstruction with acceptance" that brought me up short because it implies leaving something behind in order to learn. How does that fit with holding the line and holding on?

Ivor: That's a good point. Here I've learned a lot from feminist theorists who have written much about there having to be some deconstruction of the script that society has laid on her before a woman can fully embrace her potential selfhood. I believe that to be profoundly true in all cases. So we're back to the dialectic between social conditioning and emergent selfhood and the feminist literature was absolutely brilliant on that and on ways of knowing related to narrativity. I learned vast amounts in that period of the best feminist writing. So we're back to this issue of how you interrogate the relationship between the socially conditioned self and the emergent and potential self because my recent books are really about how people get scripted, how it's important if they are to lead an emergent and freer life for them to be able to interrogate that script, possibly deconstruct it, certainly re-formulate it, probably reconstruct it.

So the issue then is: What is that site of engagement around selfhood? What does it look like when other people come in and a dialogue begins? This is what *Narrative Pedagogy* in very early stages begins to look at. It says, "Here's a site of engagement which is people talking to each other about their narratives. This must be an important site of engagement by definition because people feel strongly about their life narratives. They've worked hard to create them, it means a lot to the way they live their lives." So if that's not a site for social engagement I don't know what is. So that seems to make that case.

But then there are all sorts of other issues coming in because, like every site of social engagement, it is layered with power. It is layered with colonising and domination-seeking moments. So both sides of the pedagogic encounter have to be hugely aware of the possibility that this could go wrong. This moment itself could be penetrated by colonising discourses. That's not an easy thing to do because—say it's talking to somebody about their work situation—you come in and the meeting is held in a university room and you walk in as the ageing bearded professor and you now want an equal discussion. It's already layered and set up to make that difficult. So one of the things that we've talked about is about how, when meeting each other, a particular vision of selfhood is embodied. One of the most tricky things particularly as you become an old lag, even an old prestigious lag, is how can you have those equality seeking moments? How can you persuade other people to suspend some of their predilections and prescribed notions about what you might be like? That gets harder and it's obviously more difficult for the other person than for you. So there are a whole set of questions here about how social situations are layered and pre-stratified and how do you suspend some of those things. That's a whole debate in itself and not one where we would come to an easy resolution either.

Yvonne: If any resolution at all, actually.

Ivor: I don't think resolution would be the right word. Some understanding might be as good as it gets but it will still be layered, stratified, and it will be a collision of different purposes. That's what every pedagogic moment is. Nonetheless it could be in my terms a *pedagogic moment*. It could be a place where both parties take away a useful learning. That's all one could hope of any encounter between human beings. So that's where narrative pedagogy starts in aspiration.

Yvonne: I have a problem with researchers who say that research should also be therapeutic. Maybe it's because I'm bolshie but the minute I hear "should" I think "why"? Although I think it can be.

Ivor: Possibly. But I would always make an important distinction—and I'm wagging my finger here—between research and therapy. They have different purposes. Take an example. We might be talking about relationships. I might note as a researcher that you're not mentioning your first husband. If I were a therapist I would probably be thinking, "Blockage, got to go there, got to get into all these strategies about denial" and so on. As a researcher I would not. I would not address this desire not to talk. I might seek some explanations of that but I would not be looking for a series of therapeutic strategies and codified bodies of knowledge that I'd bring in to resolve this issue. So there is at a certain level a distinction between the research endeavour and the therapeutic endeavour. Having said that—ha! Of course the research endeavour, the pedagogic encounter, is layered with therapeutic possibilities. It is also important for both parties to understand and be sensitive to all of the therapeutic and psychic dimensions of the encounter. A researcher who's insensitive to the psychic nature of the other is likely not to be a good researcher. So I think therapeutic sensitivity—yes, therapeutic aspects to the process—yes, are research and therapy distinct—yes.

Yvonne: That would be my view certainly but it's difficult to draw the line.

Ivor: It's difficult and it's messy. But human nature is messy.

Yvonne: And I think this is why I also have problems with some academic endeavors because they try to make a science out of people. But people are complicated. To put it in that scientific way, there are all sorts of variables. People are a mish-mash of variables.

Ivor: You can't scientise it.

Yvonne: You really can't.

Ivor: That's why I love working with Pat Sikes because she is so aware of that in every social engagement and we touch on that in *Life History in Education Settings*.[7] In some way it's gossip that we're doing. It's a very human transaction and of course it's multi-layered and of course it's partly therapeutic. Of course all that comes in and out all the time. All we are saying is that you have to be sensitive to all those things, to the messiness in every human encounter. It can go off in all sorts of dimensions. Which is why there might be an impulse to scientise it, to make it into surveys, to turn it into numbers because you thereby retreat from the messy reality. You also retreat from any chance of understanding messy human reality. That's why we're in there. Because human reality itself is messy. There's no way a research methodology could be anything other than messy if you're interested in human reality. If you're interested in something else like numbers and domination then get out of the messy reality but if you want to know about human beings you've got to climb in there and take all those chances. And of course that raises all sorts of issues because you're taking the chance as the researcher, but you are also making your "subject" take chances too so you have to be highly sensitive to ethical, therapeutic, and other variables in this.

So it is not just a messy reality we should climb into, we should climb in very carefully with great ethical concern because you are messing with somebody's selfhood and that is something to do with considerable caution. So when you say I tend to write carefully and cautiously and in a nuanced way, that's why. Because yes, both you and I are interested in understanding messy daily reality. We also recognise that we are intervening in it. And when you intervene into that it comes with some pretty big responsibilities, not only in the interaction, but when you write about it. You have to write about it in a nuanced way that represents that complexity. You cannot reduce it to a set of bullet points and orthodoxies. That's to do violence to the act. In some ways those qualitative orthodoxies are even worse than the survey numbers game in the violence they do to reality.

Yvonne: I think that's true and I have also been thinking recently about the art and craft of going into somebody's life and the way you become immersed in that and how to actually do that without trampling all over people's dreams. Because you do want to challenge. But the question is how far you go. I found that difficult in my own research when I heard stories that quite clearly did not reflect reality. Now in some ways that understanding was built on intuition, but it was intuition grounded in practice. And this is my concern with Facebook. I think we are losing the art of immersion in people's stories and lives and I think all we are going to get is the bullet points. You get the story without the chance to collaborate or locate, if you want to put it that way.

Ivor: It fascinates me that my son did research on Facebook as an identity project, that he went that way and picked up in a much more sensitive way than I would what is going on. The danger with Facebook is its little mini-scripts that people are throwing out there. Not elaborated, not terribly personalised. It's a performative self without prior internal conversation. This is the great modernist worry if you want to situate me as an old modernist. One of the virtues of a very complicated period was that modernism came with a prestige about the internal conversations people had about their plans and purposes. There are all kinds of downsides to that, but one of the good sides was, to go back to what we said about the way we operate in the world, is you get yourself organized, you work out where you are and then you go into social engagements and you move in and out. Without that internal conversation about plans and purposes I don't see what you're taking *in* to the social.

So what are you taking in to Facebook? I think what people do is they just sound off and if somebody responds to it that's somehow all them. So you put the flag up the flagpole, if somebody salutes that's me. Now that's very different from an ongoing sense of conversational selfhood about Yvonne-ness or Ivor-ness and her or his purposes, which you then take into the social milieu. So this is where we started, isn't it? We are talking about a shift in subjectivity here which fits with the needs of late capitalism for non-confrontational, consuming, empty selves. It fits Facebook and the kind of subjectivity it might sponsor. It fits beautifully with late capitalism's need for a non-interrogative subject who will consume mindlessly. Now that's too gross. Always when I make a statement I step back from it. But I always start with the gross and then work back from it but I think there is an element of truth in the gross there and we would have to re-nuance that to see whether it has any legs in terms of changes in subjectivity. I think there are changes in subjectivity. I think it's palpable, it's demographic, it's cohort-based, and we can see it playing through.

It's likely, given that iteration between social milieu and selfhood, that in a time of consumption-driven late capitalism, subjectivity will be affected. The question is, how? And the question is how demographically different that is. We suspect that new generations' subjectivity is seismically divided from where we are. We don't know but there is some evidence that that is true, which is therefore a validation for working on people's narratives as a prism to look into this. It's a good place to look into this contest. So we're back with, why are we looking at this contest now? Because we suspect, don't we, that one of the key contests at the moment in late capitalism is over people's subjectivity. It's a major site of contestation. It always is but at the moment it's of great pertinence. That's why we're there and not looking at curriculum at the moment. We might go back and look at it later but it seems to me it's the social site of greatest contestation at this point in time, so that's where I want to be.

Yvonne: But it is a social site? It isn't an individualized, private, secret site?

Ivor: No, no.

Yvonne: I think that is where there is the greatest confusion about what it is that you do because the moment you talk about subjectivity people bring all their own preconceptions to what that is and I think it's a case of repeating and reiterating the message that this is a site of contestation that resonates to the very end.

Ivor: Can we talk about that? You have hinted at it and that is people's misunderstandings but also critiques of the work. We need to talk about that because people have legitimate critiques and legitimate misapprehensions. What are they?

Yvonne: Some of them are not direct criticisms. For example, Bev Skeggs has followed Carolyn Steedman in writing about how people may be forced into telling their stories, or particular kinds of stories, and how those stories might then be appropriated. She is also critical of how stories are used to fix certain people in place so that others might become more mobile. And I suppose we could start with Gunn Imsen's critique that you tell "small stories," which they are in a way, although it's the resonances that they have and the things that have fed into that small story that elevate them. That is always part of your work, the theory of context is always there. But when you start with the story it's very easy for someone to ignore that and to ignore the context and the dialectic between them and the mechanisms of exchange and the processes by which that occurs.

Ivor: But I think we have proceeded this problem. It's not about the collection of narratives. It's about creating a life history together. And you mentioned Steedman. I have learned a great deal from her work about how this can be done. So we've seen the danger and come up with a reasonable answer to it. Nothing is a resolution but it certainly explores these issues from the right place. I've been quite surprised how little critique there's been of this kind of work. I would have thought there would have been more of a critique of the curriculum work too. But what I would like is informed and nuanced debates about these things because they are quite crucial. But that's not the way debate proceeds in the academy. It's often orthodoxy challenging and since I don't want to create an orthodoxy in the first place I think that makes me a difficult target.

Yvonne: It's also why I like the transcendent aspect of narrative, because it is a portal to looking at other things and to see, "Well what has informed this story? What has happened to make this story this way and not that way?" And then you start to think not just in terms of your own personal story. It leads to looking at the broader stage.

Ivor: It is exactly that. A portal. It is powerful for that reason. So we're back to styles of learning again. Which is that the narrative portal seems to be a very good place into pedagogy at the moment. There's an enduring search for moments. It's still determined by the pedagogic moment for the tribal groups for both of us, and the various journeys out are to understand the parameters of context it seems to me. There's this personal preoccupation with groups that we care about and how they might have a broader view of the world. And then there's our constant interrogation of the social context which makes it so difficult for them to achieve that—and we move between the two. So when you leave teaching after 12 or 13 years it's with an understanding that actually the context is so constraining that I must go out and interrogate the context now to understand why this equation is so difficult and why this conundrum cannot be solved. And it remains the correct conundrum to be curious about because we've talked about how generalisable this is for a society, for all of those embedded groups to be dis-embedded. And not, by the way, just our tribes, but the other tribes too which are similarly corralled by their context.

The tragedy of the ruling groups in England is their severely limited view of the constraints under which they operate and the contextual misapprehensions in which they're embedded. So the point we've made once but which we have to make very often is that this is about how a society functions, not just groups to whom we have particular allegiances, and rightly so. It's actually how the whole society gets ghettoised and segregated into tribal groups whose misapprehensions are total and who are embedded in their understandings of the world. So the task is dis-embedding those understandings so there is some more totalising view of the world. That's the task and that's why we move in and out of narrative, into contextual understandings, into curriculum and back again. So where you're absolutely right is to say it's not true to say I went into curriculum then moved into life history. You simply move backwards and forwards between these sites of engagement all the way through your "endless career."

Yvonne: But here is one last thing I'd like to ask before I go and it's a big thing. You have said that what we need is a thoroughgoing theory of evil. So where might we start with that?

Ivor: No, it's true. But it's a hard thing to say. We said earlier that each of the groups that we're talking about have their own psychic tragedies. Being encased in a privileged world has problems just as being excluded and deprived does. It's not just as hard, but it has its own psychic problems. But the fact is there are groups in society, elite groups who involve themselves in what is now a set of neo-liberal projects which are going to deliver widespread penury and misery to large groups in the society. Now I don't see any other way to write about that except to describe the evil elements of what is after all accumulation by dispossession. That is the mode of capital accumulation now. In that sense David Harvey's[8] right. And if the task is to make money by dispossessing various subordinate groups in the society there is no other way to conceptualise that, for me anyhow, except as a theory of evil.

For some reason, the British particularly, but many societies, are deeply opposed and uneasy with the notion that certain groups do evil things. All of history tells us that they do, and there's the famous quote about to stop evil things good men have to act. Good *men* note. I don't know what that unease about confronting evil is. You see it even in the Holocaust deniers and you see it in my own book club actually. Most of the people don't like a book that has evil within it. They find it discomfiting. So I think there's something odd about me—and we talked about our oddness as marginal observers—that beams in on the evil side of social practices because I'm very cognisant of the evil it does, particularly to some groups who happen to be my groups of choice.

But it's more than that. It's about understanding oppression and domination generally and it's about the point we have made that happy societies and happy people live best when evil is minimised. So, it's how do you control evil groups? And after all, the pursuit of profit at the expense of people's well-being is an evil. It's an evil that's endemic to a particular stage of capitalism. It is not only capitalism that delivers it. Communism delivered evil in other ways too. So I think we need specifically, historically inscribed theories of evil at particular times. One of the problems of course of writing that way is that you end up writing sociologies of loss or histories of loss. Apart from anything else nobody wants to read them and nobody wants to develop a theory of evil or embrace a theory of evil. We don't want to think there's evil in the world. For the best human reasons we don't want to confront it. The truth is and the case of the 1930s will tell you if you don't confront evil, if you don't develop a theory of evil, if you don't understand what Hitler's about, you'll get what you get. So that's the price of not theorising the evil.

Of course any common sense will tell you there's good and bad in everybody. There's evil in me and there's good in me the same as there is in you. I think understanding that evil part of us, the world, everybody, is an important part of being human. It's not the only thing we should do and certainly if we become obsessed by theories of evil it's not a route to happiness so there are all sorts of existential reasons why we don't want to concentrate on it. But I do think we need to have within our general matrix theories of evil. Yes I do. And I do think the only word you can use for some of the people, the rapacious elites that are privatising the world at the moment, is evil. They are, to use Aneurin Bevan's[9] felicitous phrase, vermin. There is no other word for that. There are verminous elements and it hurts us to say it but not to acknowledge it seems to me more fallacious.

Chapter 12

Learning and Pedagogy

Although it covers much of the same substantive and thematic ground that we have traversed in the previous two chapters, in this chapter the emphasis shifts so that we are concerned more with methodological, processual, and practical issues. In simple terms, its overarching purpose is "show, don't tell." It instantiates the pedagogical practice of fostering learning in the space created through dialogic exchange. In this respect the extracts that follow have been crafted to a greater degree than was the case in the previous chapters, although I found it surprisingly straightforward to do this. It was by no means a case of having to extract utterances from here and there and I was able to reproduce long sections of the transcript without much intervention or interference. This suggests that the learning processes I have been eager to represent here reflect rather than reconfigure those that occurred during my meeting with Ivor. I certainly went away from the meeting with the feeling that I had participated in a rich learning experience that has continued to have a bearing on my thinking since that time.

Nevertheless it would be disingenuous to imply that my intention here was anything other than to set out the ways in which ideas change shape as they are passed back and forth between conversing partners and how, in the process of exchanging words, the "third voice" referred to earlier becomes audible. This means that I selected those portions of the whole where Ivor and I change roles, where it is he who asks questions of me and where I must feel my way toward comprehension, awareness, and appreciation. This has created a chapter that has a qualitatively different "feel" to it than the previous two, not least because the emphasis on exchange and interchange means that I am a more overt presence, but also because it is more tentative in its tone.

Although my intention in this chapter is to focus on process, the subjects we discuss here are nevertheless congruent with and contribute to this purpose. Therefore I begin the conversation by alluding to the fact that I am reading around Ivor's work on narrative and in so doing I am simultaneously entering a space where I am still hesitant and uncertain and where I am feeling my way toward understanding. I am, in other words, in a space where learning can happen. The exchanges that proceed from this point of departure then go a long way to demonstrating the answers to Ivor's later question about how pedagogical moments are created. In this respect the sense of discomfort that being in a place of "unknowing" engenders in me does not come across as strongly as I would wish. At times during the exchanges that were taking place, I was overtaken by the thought that it would be easier to flee than to learn. For many members of my family fleeing, figuratively and literally, is a prominent feature of their experience of schooling and I have been thinking a great deal since meeting Ivor about why I was able, despite many difficulties, to effect that transition from wanting to absent myself to wanting to stay.

Pertinent here is our discussion of teaching and what it might mean to be a teacher. These are not intended to be normative statements but they do serve, on the one hand, as a counterpoint to emaciated notions of teachers as imparters of (examinable) knowledge. This raises questions about the implications of being a teacher if the primary purpose of the role were to be the creation of spaces in which predispositions to learning (as opposed to fleeing, for example) might be fostered. However, I must stress that our exchange here does not represent a significant contribution to discussions about the role of the teacher. Nor does it lead to any firm conclusions or plans of action. This is not its purpose. But my experience has been that it does impel further reflection. And this, I would argue, is one of the most vital aspects of any definition of learning.

Yvonne: I'm just looking at your work on narrative at the moment. I am particularly fascinated by the idea of being locked into your script. How do you break into that?

Ivor: Before we go there let's not lose the question you asked first and I want to ask you—how we have gone from a preoccupation with curriculum to the preoccupation we've just talked about, narratives and scripted realities. You are telling me in what you have written that there's a complete continuity. Tell me again what is it?

Yvonne: It's a preoccupation with how reality is created—people's life politics create a reality for them in conjunction with everything else that is going on and what you have done is focus on different sites where that is happening, which are not entirely subjective or collective.

Ivor: In fact if you look at *School Subjects and Curriculum Change* there is a lot of concern with the life histories of the main protagonists within that. So I'm not just trying to understand how the structure worked, I'm trying to understand why Sean Carson played it that way. So you're absolutely right to say that I've not moved from curriculum to life history, I've simply always been concerned with the social construction of reality in social settings. Always. That is how we get from A to B and possibly back again, isn't it?

Yvonne: That's the common thread, isn't it? I didn't want to use the words *social construction* because I didn't want to put words in your mouth. It is, but I think you have looked at that from different angles and the difficulty is that you have never been interested in one thing *or* the other. You have been interested in one thing *and* the other. It is always a "both and" position. Although you have to write about things separately to make them understandable, I have tried to make clear that this is always in the context of other things that are going on.

Ivor: It is. One of the battles I was very keen to fight in America in the 1990s when I was teaching there was the battle over what we meant by narrative because I believe that life history is the way. The life story within a theory of social context. So we are always looking at both situations. We are always looking at why is this person this way and what is the context that is partially formed and partially situated and partly allows this person to play out in this way. So it's always a dialectical relationship between self and structure. And we can have poststructuralist positions. I'm willing to embrace them. But there is always that dialectic between social context and social selfhood. And therefore I've always argued for a more complicated notion of narrative. Narrative is the buzzword of the moment and I'm happy to go with that but life history seems to me the way I really understand narrative so it's got both sides of it. It's a story of action within a theory of context—always for me. Always has been, always will be. So that battle over what we call narrative was quite a key battle in America. To get across the message that actually you can't just divorce a personal narrative from its social setting because again, thinking strategically, that would be a very easy way for power to disentangle its social structuring mechanisms from people's pursuit of their narrative understanding. And that's a good example of strategic politics, I think, seeing how power is likely to situate an emergent discourse on narrative. It will likely want to situate it as individualising, divorced from social context and so on. We have to make sure that another discourse comes into play to challenge that simplifying discourse. So there's life politics, there's prefigurative politics, and there's strategic politics, that's an example of the last.

Yvonne: My husband read one of the chapters and commented that he would have liked some flesh on Ivor's working-class bones.

Ivor: How would you do that?

Yvonne: Well, I don't know because in some ways I feel like a shadow of a working-class person myself. I still feel a particular kind of working class. I don't feel I've lost the things that were important to me then, particularly the importance of helping each other out. And the legacy of that is that I still believe you are stronger as a collective, whatever complexion you want to put on that. And I still believe in social justice for the reason that if one of us is done down so are the rest of us. But at the same time I'm not working class. I live in a nice house in a village that does not reflect the ethnic diversity of my town. I can't pretend I still feel part of the community from which I came. But I don't feel middle class. I don't have those aspirations. I don't want to be poor. I want to be comfortable—but don't want pots of money.

Ivor: Not at all. I am not working class in that sense. That's true. But in the way I view the world still, my idea of a good night out, my idea of happiness, my idea of being, comes from that. But you could certainly make a counter argument—in fact, there are many counter arguments. My range of conversation is different from the range of conversation there would be if I went back to the pub in the local village of course. Of course all of that has changed and of course it's a holding on of a sort. But it's back to your point about whether there is any continuity of purpose and position which carries you right through a life and I think there is. I think that the essential Ivor or the essential Yvonne that was formed in the cauldron of those early years has a set of values and views about the world which I continue to hold. The normal process of social mobility is to lose those and embrace a new set of values. To some degree I have done that, but by and large I don't think I have. I think my fortune, if you will, my privilege if you will, is being able to have it both ways then. Let's compromise on that. To hold to those original ideas certainly of a good night out, how to enjoy yourself, what you do in the world, whose side you're on—all of that I've been able to continue, whilst also having the benefits that are there on the other side of the social divide. So yes, it is a difficult conundrum to argue for. This is not some pure line where you remain working class throughout but it is to say you have tried to defend many of the values and joys that you found earlier whilst discarding, let's face it, some of the things you didn't like. So it's a selective holding on.

Yvonne: Yes, it is selective and we have been fortunate to have the chance and been in a position where we could reflect on what was important to us. For me that was going to university, which has made me very protective of the freedom people have to go. I'm sure I would have done well if I'd gone from school into a job. I think I would have been all right whatever I did. But I would not have learned things about myself that I did at university, about what was important to me and what my values were. Being in a different milieu also makes you question those. I don't think I would have got that in any other place.

Ivor: So are you saying we've come to hold our views and beliefs in a different way from how it would have been had we stayed put? How it is for people who are scripted early? I think that is what we are saying.

Yvonne: I think it is what I'm saying.

Ivor: So the argument is not about the positions we hold but in a sense how we hold them, how we understand them? Because of the various border crossings you have to reflexively interrogate your position—your understanding of a night out. Everything about your existence has to be reexamined during the various transitions. So in the end what you've got is a quite well-honed sense of who you are and why you are and what you want to do in the world. That seems to me to be a definition of how I would want it to be. I would want to have travelled enough through enough genres and orders to have a finely-honed sense of myself and my purposes and I find it difficult to imagine that when one is socially embedded, whether that's socially embedded at Eton or in a working-class council estate. It's about the dis-embedding process as emancipation.

Yvonne: Yes, and I think this is why since doing my research I have become more protective of the idea of access to higher education. I used to think there was far too much store set by it, that it was just one way among many and I am still in total agreement that vocational routes to employment should be equally valued. I also hate the discourse of aspiration around widening participation. I don't think people who have no desire for higher education are lacking in aspiration. But in the course of my research I came to value it as one of those border crossings. At each crossing you need to ask, shall I cross or shall I stay? And you become more flexible in your story as well. So I have become more protective of the idea that higher education should be available for all and it should be free. Because if you are already poor you are not going to get involved in something that on the face of it is going to have a still more negative effect on your financial situation. I would not have gone if that had been the case, for all you might argue it's not a debt but a graduate tax by any other name. So I think it should be for all if they want it and it should be free.

Ivor: For all but not for everyone.

Yvonne: I absolutely agree. That's a great way of putting it.

Ivor: You can see why we've ended up there in the latest book can't you? It's about flexibility of response to new transitions. For both of us there is an autobiographical element. We're reflecting on our own journey. Partly there's a celebratory aspect to it, let's be honest. Partly not. Partly we are trying to look at downsides here. Things get lost in the journey as well as gained in the journey. I think the balance sheet is one of gain but it's just the journey that suited me that's all. If you are able to go on a journey that suits you you're a lucky beggar is what it comes down to.

Yvonne: Yes. And I think that's why I am interested in Amartya Sen's[1] ideas that it's not about resources but the freedoms people have to utilize them and to actualize a life they value. Some people don't have any room for maneuver. That is what must change. Not forcing people to go to university by labelling them as lacking in aspiration if they don't, for example.

Ivor: The place to which we return is to our tribal hinterland, to the place of our own escape to ask the question again, how constrained is it for most people in that situation? And we know it to be enormously constrained and we know that the journey we went on is a privilege given to only a few and we know that that's wrong and we should know that that's wrong. And that's not driven by guilt, that's driven by an objective realization that it is wrong that people do not have a range of choices and freedoms to become who they might be in the world. That will always be a moral scandal. When you see a government rebuilding systematically those constraints not just on our tribe but other tribes we know that's wrong and we don't need to have postmodern multiple selves to know that's wrong. It's the same old story and it's the story we came here to oppose and what we came to say, you and I, is that that is wrong. That will never change. We will go to our graves saying that is wrong and whenever we can fight it we will, and in a way that is our job. Our job is to be a moral witness to the constraints on good people's realization of their potential. It's a very simple moral dilemma. I don't see it as at all complicated and I don't see the analysis of domination and oppression as at all complicated. It's nasty people doing nasty things to others. That's what the act of domination is. It doesn't have many sides. It only has one side viewed from the tribe and that is it's oppressive and it's trying to constrain people's potential. And it has to be opposed.

Yvonne: That's why I'm grateful to the present [UK] coalition government. They have brought that more to the fore. It's starting to repoliticize people and to politicize people who weren't politicized before.

Ivor: It's put us out of business in a sense because you don't need a complex nuanced view at the moment because it's so overt and so blindingly obvious and so uni-dimensional and so uniformly bad, not just for our tribe but for the whole swathe of professional tribes as well. Talk about hegemonic over-reach. These people are trying to deprofessionalize the professional classes. How stupid can you be to take on the doctors and nurses and even the lawyers? It's gone ballistic. If you look at history this is an example of systematic overreach. When you take on the professional classes history tells you, you fall in the end. You can normally dominate the proletariat, you can normally dominate the peasantry, you can normally dominate our tribes. When you take on other levels as well you really are behaving stupidly. So I think this is an incredibly interesting time.

Yvonne: It feels interesting.

Ivor: It is interesting but it's also awful. It is both. It's a privilege to say it's interesting as a social scientist but we are also aware it's appalling in what it's doing to the potential routes for our tribes. It's emasculating. We also have to break down interesting. It's interesting because it appears to be over-reaching itself. It appears to be possible that this project of domination might self-destruct. So there are material aspects to it being interesting here. It is interesting, for example, that comprehensives have been brought back in as somehow other than bog standard and awful. They have been reinspired as desirable experiments in human nature.

Yvonne: Both my boys went to the local comp and though I get it in some ways, it breaks my heart when people send their kids to selective schools or fee-paying schools instead of doing that. That's where you learn that not everyone has the same kind of life as you do. And in particular that some people have lives that are so much harder for no good reason.

Ivor: As a place of education for the things we are talking about those are sites of engagement that were rich and the disvaluing and destruction of those for whatever reason is criminal. There is no other word for it. This is social cruelty of epic proportions to destroy them. I find it indescribably awful what's being done in the name of standards and excellence.

Yvonne: And standards and excellence in what? What are we being excellent in? Some important, possibly counterfactual questions are not being asked. Why have six kids from my hometown been killed in Afghanistan, for example, including someone my son was friends with at primary school? My son decided not to go to his funeral, despite the genuine grief felt, because he did not want his presence to be taken as acquiescence in the discourses around that—the valorization of the "sacrifice" and so on. And that makes me ask, "Why is it not possible just to grieve here? Why are straightforward human emotions being distorted in such a way?" These are philosophical questions on one level, but they can also be tackled through the curriculum, through research, history will come into it and so on. Why is it so terrible if things are not being taught the way they were?

Ivor: What they are saying is, "Why are things not taught in the way they were in the public school I went to?"[2] So we're back in the old terrain we started in. The way that the social battle is being fought, is to narrow learning and education back to a very traditional core that resonates with public and grammar school curricula and which ensure that that group succeed and the other group don't. So we're back in a battle where we started.

Yvonne: I think everything has come back.

Ivor: Pretty much. Pretty much back to the original struggle. It's gone in a huge circle with the same ruling class back in order that we thought for a while had been dissolved. In a sense we're back to the 1950s. A group are in charge we thought had gone away then, but didn't.

Yvonne: They were just regrouping.

Ivor: The public schools are stronger now than they have been for decades.

Yvonne: And other types of school, independent schools, private schools, and academies and the like, are proliferating because people don't want to send their children to comprehensive schools because they have a view, for right or wrong, that comprehensives are a certain kind of place.

Ivor: I suppose it comes back to this battle about the definition of what is learning and what is education, because if you define it in a particular way then comprehensives are set up to fail. To go back to the battle over curriculum—that was the battle. By narrowing the battle over comprehensives to the battle over curriculum they essentially built in failure to the comprehensive experiment because they said, "OK you can have all the pupils there but they've got to learn this particular sort of thing." Once that happened the experiment could not proceed in any way that was open. So the experiment was closed with inevitable consequences.

Yvonne: It was never entirely comprehensive—it was two systems under one roof. But if it is to work you can't have that.

Ivor: Then you need comprehensive curricula. You can't have grammar school curricula in comprehensive schools. You are going to regress in the end.

Yvonne: It will create a tension that will pull it apart. It can't not. I find it really frustrating that we serve up such a boring diet to people who could really get excited about things.

Ivor: But that boring diet has a purpose which is reproduction of the social order. In one sense it has to be so for that system to work. For the system to work a certain group has to be bored into failure. Born into failure and bored into failure. That's the tragedy. But going back to your son's reflexivity on the issue of the funeral, we were lucky enough to be able to polish up our reflexivity, to put it humorously. What intrigues me is the question of how we find a way for the next generation, born into a different situation, possibly born into the centre of scripts, to be as reflexive. How do we keep creating pedagogic moments like the ones we were lucky enough to have in our border crossing lives? How do you fit those into lives that are maybe more settled, more frozen, more constrained? This is the social question, isn't it? That's why for the moment I'm interested in these narrative differences because they return to that question of how constrained groups can nonetheless find ways through into different zones of understanding. Otherwise it's just a freezing of the social situation in ways that certainly don't help our tribes but I don't think helps society generally. This is not just a sort of leftist agenda. This is actually an agenda about how you have social understanding generally because it's no more desirable to have a constrained person as prime minister than it is to have a constrained person in a working-class community. To have people in both places who don't understand the wider context is equally bad. And actually equally sad for both parties. I think it must be awful to be in this situation where the only discourse you can come up with is some fatuous big society, one which everybody laughs at, you can't create a story for love nor money, nobody believes in any of the narratives you construct, you're a laughing stock when you do. That's rather hard for someone who thinks they'll be rather good at this job but finds out they're actually useless at it.

Yvonne: That's the point though, isn't it, Ivor? That actually nobody wins. Either everybody wins or nobody actually wins and to me that's such an obvious point.

Ivor: I discovered that in South Africa. That's going further down the road of privileged domination than we've got. When you move into a society and you live as we did among the rich white areas you realize they weren't winning either. There was this horrendous paranoid existence of no joy to anyone. OK they'd cornered all the resources but it's like the rich in gated communities in other parts of the world. This is not a win situation, this is a paranoid blocking off of the gates.

Yvonne: Yes, and you've been to Brazil where it's the same. People cowering behind iron gates. What kind of existence is that? That's not freedom for anybody. What kind of story must you have been scripted into to not get that obvious point?

Ivor: Let's try and be anthropological about this. In the same way that we were born into tribal understandings of the sort that we've just talked about—nights out and the various existential patterns that are part of tribal understanding—in the same way, ruling groups are born into that tribal understanding. And their tribal understanding is clearly that they're born to rule, they're born to dominate their inferiors and that is their holy mission. That is their understanding of the world and that's what is ingrown into them. What is specifically left out of most of it is the kind of argument that you see in the *Spirit Level*[3] and other things which says, actually, the happiest societies are those who share, who do not have this rigid class definition that we have in England. There is no more rigid and ossified class structure anywhere in the world than here. To have a whole elite dominated by a few schools and for all the resources, all the legal jobs, all the serious journalistic jobs, dominated by that group is a form of class domination of a quite astonishingly concentrated kind.

Now of course when you're in that tribal elite, I'm sure it feels like you're doing the right thing by your tribe, the same way we want to do the right thing by our tribe. What we are saying is, if you could just develop a theory of context beyond your tribe, whichever tribe we're talking about, then you would see the essential human truth, that the happiest societies are the ones where there is a degree of sharing across the social order and where people try to live in reasonable equanimity together. That's the clear message of the world. And yet, these elites are lining up with an economic system, neo-liberalism, which concentrates wealth and power increasingly in very small, rapacious global elites and leaves most of the people, not just our tribe but the professional tribes too, outside the gates. That is a prescription for gross social unhappiness and gross social unrest. I would say what I've just said is empirically highly defensible and yet I can understand why the tribal groups at the top of society don't buy it. And yet they are wrong not to. It's a failure of imagination on their part. As it was a failure of imagination on the part of the white elites in South Africa to think that domination would lead to happiness. It led to gross unhappiness among them all and in the end to social breakdown and the same thing will happen here. And the same thing will happen across Europe if they go on with this pernicious experiment.

Yvonne: Does it always have to get so bad before it gets better?

Ivor: I think so. Look at South Africa. Look at how bad it got. It got to the point where you were having to shoot people to hold it. Look at Syria. Look at Bahrain. It has to get that bad and we're not close.

Yvonne: It feels bad though. Maybe it hasn't become a group or collective thing but certainly some people are finding it difficult to survive and actually are not surviving it. Suicide rates are up.

Ivor: But I suppose elites would say that's all manageable problems. If we're not having to kill people on the streets.

Yvonne: So, as long as it's a "private" matter . . .

Ivor: OK there's a lot of mental health problems and there's a lot of deprivation in the areas we never go to, but frankly that's quite manageable. That's what they would say, wouldn't they, Yvonne? We've got large armies and large police forces, we can manage a little bit of low level disease and depression among certain groups. That's where we are. So I'm not so hopeful.

Yvonne: Then again there are whole swathes of society that are being medicated into docility.

Ivor: Like Ritalin in America. But again manageable and remember we've got the largest prison population in Europe. That's one big growth area. But you know it's not just conservative politicians. Let's be balanced about it. It's rapacious elites across the globe. And they come on both sides of the political divide. So when I said that it's a tribal thing, I'm saying it's the same for both tribes really. It's simply true that it's a mistake not to go for a more equal distribution of money. It's a mistake I would say just in cold economic terms and remember most of my training is in economic history. The problem with the depression was that there was not enough demand because the people that buy the most are the poor not the rich. Once you start pushing austerity down on to the poor who are the best consumers you're simply starving demand and making things worse.

So this rapacious elite that wants to punish the poor will end up punishing itself. This failure of understanding of tribal groups whether they be ruling class or another is disastrous for society. When a society stops the kind of social critique that we're talking about, it stops being reflexive about itself, and when it stops being reflexive about itself it's essentially doomed in the medium term. This society has stopped being reflexive about itself because it fears reflexivity. It's making education more mundane and subject-focused. It's trying to trivialise most of the things that come out from the BBC and the media. All of those things make reflexivity less rather than more likely and therefore survival less rather than more likely. That's the truth.

Yvonne: It is, and I think this is why I refer to it as an art and a craft. It's not something that just happens. It takes a certain amount of practice and a certain sensibility. And this is teaching, isn't it? We're talking about being a teacher in its widest sense and this is also why I'm glad I had Pat Sikes as a supervisor. I feel the same about that. In all kinds of ways I am a completely different kind of researcher because of Pat.

Ivor: You were lucky.

Yvonne: I was extremely fortunate. She has been a teacher in the broadest sense.

Ivor: But that's the kind of iconic role of Pat or us in our better moments. It's not just the individual intervention, it's seeing modelled the way to do the business and I suppose what we would hope we're seeing ourselves do is modelling that capacity to know when to intervene and how to catch the moment with people and it has a lot of things about it. You can think of the way Pat's embodied so to speak. There's a whole package of personal orientation and personality here which works for people or doesn't. I've tried to analyse it often, how you can get into those relationships with people. How you can undercut the socially embedded nature of the situation and the power relations of the thing. There is something about the way you present yourself to the world that helps that—in Pat's case for sure. She fronts up as a human being. She doesn't hide behind her role at all. And that's part of it I think.

Yvonne: I didn't have to pretend with Pat. I could go into it as myself and do what I wanted to do. I didn't have to act the role of somebody researching. Because I was so glad to be doing it—I waited a long time for it—I didn't want to do anything that would jeopardize that. I didn't want to step out of line. But with Pat the line was my line. I didn't have to worry I was doing something wrong.

Ivor: I suspect with disadvantaged groups generally the only way it works is if that personal threshold is played that way. In other words the teacher, the pedagogue, whoever, has to create a space where Yvonne can be Yvonne without playing the roles which we've learned to distrust. So I always felt in a classroom as a teacher the knack was to suspend most of the normal teacherly roles in the name of not laying on the disadvantaged kids a set of roles they had been trained to distrust and therefore I tried to communicate over the space, as just people having a good time. That was my idea. I was trying in the classroom to replicate this romance we've talked about. It's got to be fun was my starting point. The only way these kids are going to learn is if this is fun, if you have a laugh and they tease you and there's jokes and they're not seen to be working. Therefore they're not caught learning in front of their mates and girlfriends—it was a mixed classroom. They're playing around, the girls and boys are having fun. Because if you're caught learning, that's out.

And I remember trying to explain that to the other teachers because the other teachers would say, "You're not serious about learning, Ivor. Every time I go past your classroom there's howls of laughter and chaos." And I used to try and say, "Yeah, but if you're going to reach these kids from this tough estate, the conventional way does not work." And this is what Gove has to understand. You can battle over what kind of knowledge but it's not a public school where everybody's sitting in lines and they're predetermined to learn. This is a battle ground where most of the people who are turning up don't believe in the game. That's the starting point. So you can tighten the rules, you can do what you like with your "A" levels. They don't believe in the game so you've got to change the space in dramatic ways. So all the advice you're given as a teacher trainee is completely wrong. For example, one piece of advice is never smile before Christmas. If you're trying to create a fun environment in a classroom that's complete kiss of death because the first thing every working-class kid does is test you out and tease you to see if you can take it and to see if you can make it stick. You have to discipline them. You have to say, "OK that's enough now." And you have to have that look which says, "No more of this." Once you've given them that look and they've bought it, no more discipline problems.

However, having created a fun space the task then is to create serious pedagogic moments. That's the really tricky bit because somehow you've created a space here that has suspended all the expectations, but actually you're still a teacher with expectations so you have to smuggle in the learning, to hook them in a way that my teacher did with me. And in the end most people are interested in learning something some time. But it's about suspending most of the rules that are out there because those are the rules of domination. Those are the rules that aim to get people to learn to labour. The game is to fail certain groups. That's the truth and those people being failed know that's the game, so it's no use tightening the rules because they know what the game is. That's a very deviant view but it's true. We've been inside the classroom we know that's true. You approach school with a sense of fear and loathing. I remember walking through our village to school, and I didn't go till I was 6, and kids were screaming, hanging on to the backs of their mum's bikes at the prospect of going because they know you're going to waste all these years in school and then you're going to end up in a factory. What's the point? What you're going to do is try and make school as much fun and games as it can be because it's an interlude before penury. It's nothing else. It's not a gateway to the heavens for most kids. It's a gateway to the factory, or was. It's a gateway to sod all now. So you're not going to apply yourself, are you? So the teacher's task is to say, "OK, that's the game. We're here for fun and games. Let's have some and smuggle in the learning."

Yvonne: I was never a very good teacher. I was a good teacher in some ways, but I never really got the idea about how you could do that. I had every sympathy with the people who were sitting there, that it was irrelevant to them, but my way was to say, "Just rise above this, play the game in an ironic way." But I think that was the wrong way. I think a better way would have been to do the smuggling. I tried to get them to reflect too much on different ways of playing the game.

Ivor: But I don't think I was a great teacher either. I don't make that claim.

Yvonne: I had some successes, some things I was proud of.

Ivor: I had some kids definitely that no other teacher got to. But I think I paid quite a price in terms of being seen as an irresponsible funster—and I was an irresponsible funster. I was both. It was not a perfect game at all.

Yvonne: But I think that's the terrible thing. The game becomes bigger than anything you can do about it. I also found it so difficult to have my kids in school. Because I felt for them so much. And I think I did with my own kids what I did with classrooms full of kids, which was to try and get them to reflect more on the game. I think one-to-one it worked a lot better, and also because I was their parent they listened more. So I think I had more success there. But I actually start to sweat when I drive past a secondary school. I break out in a cold sweat.

Ivor: Because?

Yvonne: Because it just brings back how hard it was to teach in one. To be concerned about the future of these children but feeling totally out of your depth about how to approach it. All the time I was teaching, and I taught for a long time, I felt out of my depth.

Ivor: I can relate to that absolutely. [Ivor looks through *Identity and Schooling*][5] I'm just looking for this one thing you know—about the dream I have.

Yvonne: About being at the staff party?

Ivor: Yes. I had that dream again and again. That was my experience of school. I was looking from inside the tribe still. Still a working-class kid in a way. And so I looked at school the same way the kids did. With the same, in a sense, hostility. How long did you teach for?

Yvonne: For 12, 13 years. And in a way you know—this has just come to me—I went in thinking I could make a difference and that I could actually change things and that I would actually have an effect. And then when I didn't, I found it really hard to take. I suppose I was really idealistic.

Ivor: How long did your ideals last?

Yvonne: I suppose the idealism lasted . . . I suppose it was just the last couple of years where I gave up. And then it becomes a kind of plodding thing.

Ivor: Why did you give up?

Yvonne: I think I just came to the realization that no, you're not going to make a difference, no, you're not going to change things from the inside, no, this is far bigger than you. Whatever made you think you could? Plus I had my own children, so this is where the life politics comes in. I had different concerns then. I couldn't give my all to this institution, to these kids, because I had these other kids right here and I had to do things with them as well and I had to give them my attention.

Ivor: That's the normal life cycle of a teacher, isn't it? I think there's that innovative moment when you give it your all and during that moment you can suspend context to a degree.

Yvonne: Well, for a long time I saw my whole teaching career and the fact I left it in the end as a personal failure. This is why it's so important to have that contextual element as well because you can start to broaden it out.

Ivor: Context is set up to do what we don't want it to do.

Yvonne: I've got to watch the time so I don't miss my train.

Ivor: Go on, look at your list, make sure you have covered it all.

Yvonne: No, no. I had a quick look before when you went out to get a sandwich and we've covered it all and more. You're dead right. Everything has kind of been covered without me having to read off the sheet.

Ivor: Did I say that to you?

Yvonne: Yes, you did, and you're dead right.

Ivor: Oh, good.

Yvonne: Thanks ever so much. I know you like the dialogic exchange but I'm sure you must get terribly fed up of people coming and wanting to have these conversations.

Ivor: No, I don't actually. That's the awful thing. Because they are after all what we said—they're pedagogic moments. You always learn something.

Concluding Remarks

Although I have now come to the end of the line I have pursued through *Reading and Teaching Ivor Goodson*, I have no sense of having offered a comprehensive representation of Ivor's life/work. In terms of subject matter, for example, there are many aspects of Ivor's scholarship that I have not visited or done so only fleetingly. Most important among these are his contributions to social policy, his work as a publisher and its contribution to his public intellectual role, and the significance of his transnational perspective. Therefore, had it been my intention to package Ivor between the covers of this book so that he might be understood here, I would now be found wanting.

But I would have been found wanting in any case. As consistent and coherent as I found the man and his concerns and preoccupations, both in the reading and the meeting, he is all too aware of shifts and changes on the broader sociopolitical stage and their potential to reposition the import of his work. He could not remain unresponsive to them or complacent about the meaning of his scholarship. It would, in short, be impossible to pin him down once and for all. His continued and prolific published output alone would militate against this.

Therefore, while the questions he asks today are still fired by his desire not only to understand but also to change understandings of the social world, he moves continuously in and out of those sites of engagement, according to where he might best pursue these ambitions. The idea that he might be frozen in time and space or captured between the pages of a book is antithetical to his own way of going about things. And yet there are certain leitmotifs running through his life/work regardless of his location: his foregrounding of personal life politics, which in his case comprises a complex amalgamation of the personal and broader socio-historical influences; the commitment to social justice; his loyalty to his tribe; his dedication to the role of public intellectual; his methodological allegiance to life history, even in the study of narrative and the mechanisms of narrative production; and his insistence that theory should have resonance in, relevance to, and impact on material realities. These serve not as a reductive summation of his life/work but indicate instead a moral position to which he has held for most of his life.

In keeping with the aims of the series, what I have offered here is neither a *reading of* Ivor Goodson nor a *way to read* Ivor Goodson. It is instead an interpretation of the significance of his life/work to educational endeavor and provides a portal to deeper insight into it. My overarching hope for the book is simply that some of the vitality, joy, and optimism with which Ivor infuses his scholarship might have somehow seeped into my writing of him so that his ideas might resonate with, reinvigorate, and reinspire the life politics and socio-personal projects of those who are concerned with the creation of pedagogic moments and of a reimagined and just social life.

Notes to Teaching Ivor Goodson

Notes for Biography

1. Schools that follow a "traditional" academic curriculum and that select their intake, usually through administering some form of entrance examination.
2. A film written by Alan Bennett and directed by Nicholas Hytner about a group of boys who are being taught history in preparation for the entrance exam to Oxford.
3. Abbreviation of *secondary modern*, schools to which the majority of pupils in England went before introduction of comprehensives.
4. Local squires in the area in which Ivor was born.

Notes for Scholarship

1. Reference to the Hillsborough Inquiry into events at the ground of Sheffield Wednesday Football Club in 1989 that led to the deaths of 96 Liverpool supporters. The inquiry has provided strong support that police and the football club actively and wrongly sought to divert responsibility for the deaths onto the fans themselves and led to the success of a long struggle by the families of the deceased for fresh inquests into the deaths.
2. A well-known celebrity in the UK who in 2012 was posthumously exposed as a paedophile and sex offender amid suspicion that he had "hidden in plain view" and that the BBC had long colluded in keeping knowledge of his conduct out of the public domain.
3. A "grassroots movement taking action to highlight alternatives to the government's spending cuts" (www.ukuncut.org.uk).
4. Inter alia, Bauman (2000).
5. Salmon (2010).
6. Michael Gove, Secretary of State for Education in the Coalition Government of the UK.
7. Goodson and Sikes (2001).

8. Distinguished Professor of Anthropology and Geography at the Graduate Center of the City University of New York and Director of the Center for Place, Culture and Politics (http://davidharvey.org).

9. Welsh Labour politician and architect of the National Health Service who stated in 1948 that "no amount of cajolery, and no attempts at ethical or social seduction, can eradicate from my heart a deep burning hatred for the Tory Party that inflicted those bitter experiences on me. So far as I am concerned they are lower than vermin".

Notes for Learning and Pedagogy

1. Amartya Sen, economist and Nobel Laureate whose "Capability Approach" foregrounds the freedoms people enjoy to live lives they value rather than measures such as GDP in evaluations of the success of economic policy.

2. In England "public schools" are in fact elite, private, fee-paying schools.

3. Wilkinson and Pickett (2009).

4. Goodson and Walker (1991).

References

Bateson, G. (1972). *Steps to an ecology of mind*. San Francisco: Chandler.

Bauman, Z. (2000). *Liquid modernity*. Cambridge: Polity Press.

Berlant, L. (1997). *The queen of America goes to Washington*. Durham, NC: Duke University Press.

Biesta, G., Field, J., Hodkinson, P., Macleod, F., & Goodson, I. (2011). *Improving learning through the lifecourse: Learning lives*. London: Routledge.

Blunkett, D. (2000). Influence or irrelevance? Can social science improve government? Speech to the Economic and Social Research Council, February 2 2000. *Research Intelligence, 71*, 12–21.

Booker, C. (2006). *The seven basic plots: Why we tell stories*. London: Continuum.

Breines, W. (1980). Community and organization: The new left and Michel's "Iron Law." *Social Problems, 27*(4), 496–506.

Caldwell, C. (2005, November 18). The final round for party politics. *The Financial Times*.

Callaghan, J. (1976). Towards a national debate. Speech given at Ruskin College, Oxford, October 18. Retrieved from http://education.guardian.co.uk/thegreatdebate/story/0,9860,574645,00.html

Cox, C. B., & Dyson A. E. (Eds.). (1969a). *Fight for education: A black paper*. London: The Critical Quarterly Society.

————(1969b). *Black paper two: The crisis in education*. London: The Critical Quarterly Society.

Frank, A. (1995). *The wounded storyteller: Body, illness and ethics*. Chicago: Chicago University Press.

Giddens, A. (1991). *Modernity and self-identity: Self and society in the late modern age*. Cambridge: Polity Press.

Goodson, I. (1980–1981). Life histories and the study of schooling. *Interchange, 11*(4), 62–76.

————(1981). Becoming an academic subject. *British Journal of Sociology of Education, 2*(2), 163–180.

————(1983). *School subjects and curriculum change*. London: Croom Helm.

————(1984). Subjects for study. Towards a social history of curriculum. In I. Goodson & S. Ball (Eds.), *Defining the curriculum: Histories and ethnographies* (pp. 25–44). London: Falmer.

————(1985). Towards curriculum history. In I. Goodson (Ed.), *Social histories of the secondary curriculum: Subjects for study.* (pp. 1-8). London: Falmer.

————(1987). *School subjects and curriculum change* (3rd ed.). London: Falmer.

————(1988). *International perspectives in curriculum history*. London: Routledge.

————(1989). Curriculum reform and curriculum theory: A case of historical amnesia. *Cambridge Journal of Education, 19*(2), 131–141.

————(1990a). Curriculum history: Knowledge and professionalization. *Curriculum and Teaching, 5*(1&2), 3–13.

————(1990b). "Nations at risk" and "National Curriculum": Ideology and identity. *Journal of Education Policy, 5*(5), 219–232.

————(1990c). Subjects for study: Research agenda. *Journal of Curriculum and Supervision,* *21*(1), 35–45.

————(1991a). Sponsoring the teacher's voice. *Cambridge Journal of Education, 21*(1), 35–45.

————(1991b). School subjects: Patterns of change. *Curriculum and Teaching, 6*(1), 3–11.

————(1992a). School subjects: Patterns of stability. *Education Research and Perspectives,* *19*(1), 52–64.

————(1992b). School subjects: The context of cultural inventions. *Curriculum & Teaching,* *7*(2), 47–58.

————(1992c). *Studying teachers' lives.* London: Routledge.

————(1994). *Studying curriculum: Cases and methods.* Buckingham: Open University Press.

————(1995). *The making of curriculum: Collected essays* (2nd ed.). London: Falmer.

————(1997a). "Trendy theory" and teacher professionalism. *Cambridge Journal of Education, 27*(l), 7–22.

————(1997b). Representing teachers. *Teaching and Teacher Education: An International Journal of Research and Studies, 13*(1), 111–117.

————(1997c). *The changing curriculum: Studies in social construction.* New York: Peter Lang.

————(1999). The educational researcher as a public intellectual. *British Educational Research Journal, 25*(3), 277–297.

————(2003). *Professional knowledge, professional lives: Studies in education and change.* Maidenhead: Open University Press.

————(2005a). *Learning, curriculum, life politics: The selected works of Ivor F. Goodson.* London: Routledge.

————(2005b). Long waves of educational reform: Extract from "Report to the Spencer Foundation." In I. Goodson (Ed.), *Learning curriculum, life politics* (pp. 105–129). London: Routledge.

————(2006, Fall). The rise of the life narrative. *Teacher Education Quarterly,* pp. 7–21.

————(2007). All the lonely people: The struggle for private meaning and public purpose in education. *Critical Studies in Education, 48*(3), 131–148.

————(2008). *Investigating the teacher's life and work.* Rotterdam: Sense.

————(2009a). Developing life and work histories of teachers. *Journal of Applied Research in Education, 13*, 1–13.

————(2009b). Personal history and curriculum study. In E. Short & L. Waks (Eds.), *Leaders in curriculum studies: Intellectual self-portraits* (pp. 91–104). Rotterdam: Sense.

————(2011). *Life politics: Conversations about education and culture.* Rotterdam: Sense.

————(2013). *Developing narrative theory.* London: Routledge.

————(in press). *Education, personal narrative and the social future.* London: Routledge.

Goodson, I., & Anstead, C. (2010). *Through the schoolhouse door.* Rotterdam: Sense.

Goodson, I., Anstead, C., & Mangan, M. (1998). *Subject knowledge: Readings for the study of school subjects.* London: Falmer.

Goodson, I., & Ball, S. (Eds.). (1984). *Defining the curriculum: Histories and ethnographies.* London: Falmer.

————(1989). *Teachers' lives and careers.* London: Falmer/Open University Press.

Goodson, I., Biesta, G., Tedder, M., & Adair, N. (2010). *Narrative learning.* London: Routledge.

Goodson, I., & Deakin Crick, R. (2009). Curriculum as narration: Tales from the children of the colonized. *The Curriculum Journal, 20*(3), 225–236.

Goodson, I., & Gill, S. (2011). *Narrative pedagogy.* New York: Peter Lang.

Goodson, I., & Hargreaves, A. (Eds.). (1996). *Teachers' professional lives.* London: Falmer.

Goodson, I., Knobel, M., Lankshear, C., & Mangan, M. (2002). *Cyber spaces/social spaces: Culture clash in computerized classrooms.* New York: Palgrave Macmillan.

Goodson, I., & Lindblad, S. (Eds.). (2011). *Professional knowledge and educational restructuring in Europe.* Rotterdam: Sense.

Goodson, I., & Marsh, C. (1996). *Studying school subjects: A guide.* London Falmer.

Goodson, I., & Sikes, P. (2001). *Life histories in educational settings: Learning from lives.* Buckingham: Open University Press.

Goodson, I., & Walker, R. (1991). *Biography, identity and schooling: Episodes in educational research.* Basingstoke: Falmer.

Hargreaves, A. (1994). Introduction. In I. Goodson (Ed.), *Studying curriculum: Cases and methods* (pp. 1–11). Buckingham: Open University Press.

Harvey, D. (1990). *The condition of postmodernity.* Oxford: Blackwell.

HMI (1983). *Teacher quality.* London: HMSO.

Hoggart, R. (1958). *The uses of literacy.* Harmondsworth: Penguin.

Issa, T., & Pick, D. (2010). Ethical mindsets: An Australian study. *Journal of Business Ethics, 96*(4), 613–629.

Kincheloe, J. (1997). Introduction. In I. Goodson (Ed.), *The changing curriculum: Studies in social construction* (pp. ix–xl). New York: Peter Lang.

Krugman, P. (2012). *End this depression now.* New York: Norton.

Layton, D. (1973). *Science for the people: The origins of the school science curriculum in England.* London: Allen and Unwin.

Lury, C. (1998). *Prosthetic culture: Photography, memory and identity.* London: Routledge.

Mahoney, P., & Zmroczek, C. (1997). Introduction. In P. Mahoney & C. Zmorczek (Eds.), *Class matters: "Working class" women's perspectives on social class* (pp. 1–7). Abingdon: Taylor and Francis.

Mills, C. W. (1959). *The sociological imagination.* New York: Oxford University Press.

Moreira A. (2007). Apresentação *Educação Em Revista, 45.* Retrieved from http://www.scielo.br/scielo.php?script=sci_arttext&pid=S0102-46982007000100006&lng=es&nrm=iso&tlng=pt

Moriarty, J. (2012). *Autobiographical and research experiences with academic writings: An analytical ethnodrama.* Brighton: University of Brighton.

Mortimer, E. (2007). Da história das disciplinas ao mundo do ensino: entrevista com Ivor Goodson. *Educação Em Revista, 45.* Retrieved from http://www.scielo.br/scielo.php?script=sci_arttext&pid=S0102-46982007000100007&lng=es&nrm=iso&tlng=pt

Pinar, W. (1995). Introduction. In I. Goodson, (Ed.), *The making of curriculum: Collected essays* (2nd ed; pp. xix–xxi). London: Falmer.

Plummer, K. (1995). *Telling sexual stories: Power, change and social worlds.* New York: Routledge.

Polkinghorne, D. (1995). Narrative configuration in qualitative analysis. In A. Hatch & R. Wisniewski (Eds.), *Life history and narrative* (pp. 5–23). London: Falmer.

Salmon, C. (2010). *Storytelling: Bewitching the modern mind.* London: Verso.

Sayer, A. (2011). *Why things matter to people: Social science, values and ethical life.* Cambridge: Cambridge University Press.

Sikes, P. (1997). *Parents who teach: Stories from home and from school.* London: Cassell.

————(2011). Talking lives. A conversation about life history: Using the content of a conversation between Ivor Goodson and Barry Troyna. In I. Goodson (Ed.), *Life politics: Conversations about culture and education* (pp. 15–30). Rotterdam: Sense.

Skeggs, B. (1997). *Formations of class and gender: Becoming respectable.* London: Sage.

————(2004). *Class, self, culture.* London: Routledge.

Sparkes, A. (2009). Novel ethnographic representations and the dilemmas of judgement. *Ethnography and Education, 4*(3), 301–319.

Steedman, C. (1986). *Landscape for a good woman.* London: Virago.

————(2000). Enforced narratives: Stories of another self. In T. Cosslett, C. Lury, & P. Summerfield (Eds.), *Feminism and autobiography: Texts, theories, methods* (pp. 25–39). London: Routledge.

Stenhouse, L. (1975). *An introduction to curriculum research and development.* London: Heinemann.

Walker, R. (1973). Teaching that's a joke. SAFARI Occasional Paper 4, University of East Anglia.

Wilkinson, R., & Pickett, K. (2009). *The spirit level: Why greater equality makes societies stronger.* New York: Bloomsbury.

Žižek, S. (2008, March 19). *Embedded in ideology.* Keynote address at the Discourse, Power Resistance conference. Manchester Metropolitan University.

Index

⟨◉Ʋ𝑁ⱦΣRƤ◉I𝑁ⱦꙄ ▶⟩

Studies in the Postmodern Theory of Education

General Editor
Shirley R. Steinberg

Counterpoints publishes the most compelling and imaginative books being written in education today. Grounded on the theoretical advances in criticalism, feminism, and postmodernism in the last two decades of the twentieth century, Counterpoints engages the meaning of these innovations in various forms of educational expression. Committed to the proposition that theoretical literature should be accessible to a variety of audiences, the series insists that its authors avoid esoteric and jargonistic languages that transform educational scholarship into an elite discourse for the initiated. Scholarly work matters only to the degree it affects consciousness and practice at multiple sites. Counterpoints' editorial policy is based on these principles and the ability of scholars to break new ground, to open new conversations, to go where educators have never gone before.

For additional information about this series or for the submission of manuscripts, please contact:

Shirley R. Steinberg
c/o Peter Lang Publishing, Inc.
29 Broadway, 18th floor
New York, New York 10006

To order other books in this series, please contact our Customer Service Department:

(800) 770-LANG (within the U.S.)
(212) 647-7706 (outside the U.S.)
(212) 647-7707 FAX

Or browse online by series:
www.peterlang.com